# BLUEWATER FISHING

## Julie & Lawrie McEnally

AFN
AUSTRALIAN FISHING NETWORK

Fully Revised edition 2006
First published in 1998 by
Australian Fishing Network Pty Ltd
48 Centre Way, South Croydon, VIC 3136
Telephone: (03) 9761 4044
Facsimile: (03 9761 4055
Email: sales@afn.com.au
Website: www.afn.com.au

Copyright © Julie & Lawrie McEnally and
Australian Fishing Network 2006

Front Cover photograph by David Granville
Designed by: Joy Eckermann
Illustrations by: Trevor Hawkins and Julie McEnally
Knots by: Geoff Wilson

ISBN 186513 085 0

This book is copyright. Except for the purpose of fair reviewing, no part of this publication may be reproduced or transmitted in any form or by any means, electronic or mechanical, including photocopying, recording, or any information storage and retrieval system, without permission in writing from the publisher. Infringers of copyright render themselves liable to prosecution.

# Contents

|  | Introduction | 1 |
|---|---|---|
| Chapter 1 | The Boat—The Fishing Vehicle | 3 |
| Chapter 2 | Tackle | 13 |
| Chapter 3 | Finding Fish | 33 |
| Chapter 4 | Lure Trolling for Big Game Fish | 41 |
| Chapter 5 | Trolling for Small Game Fish | 53 |
| Chapter 6 | Trolling Baits | 57 |
| Chapter 7 | Sharks | 69 |
| Chapter 8 | Inshore Trolling | 73 |
| Chapter 9 | Lure Casting | 77 |
| Chapter 10 | Saltwater Fly Fishing | 83 |
| Chapter 11 | Jigging | 85 |
| Chapter 12 | Drift Fishing | 89 |
| Chapter 13 | Fishing at Anchor | 97 |
| Chapter 14 | Bottom and Reef Fishing | 105 |
| Chapter 15 | Hooking and Fighting Fish | 111 |
| Chapter 16 | Live Baits—Catching and Rigging | 121 |
| Chapter 17 | Enjoying the Catch | 129 |
| Chapter 18 | Species | 132 |
|  | Appendix—Five Most Common Knots | 139 |

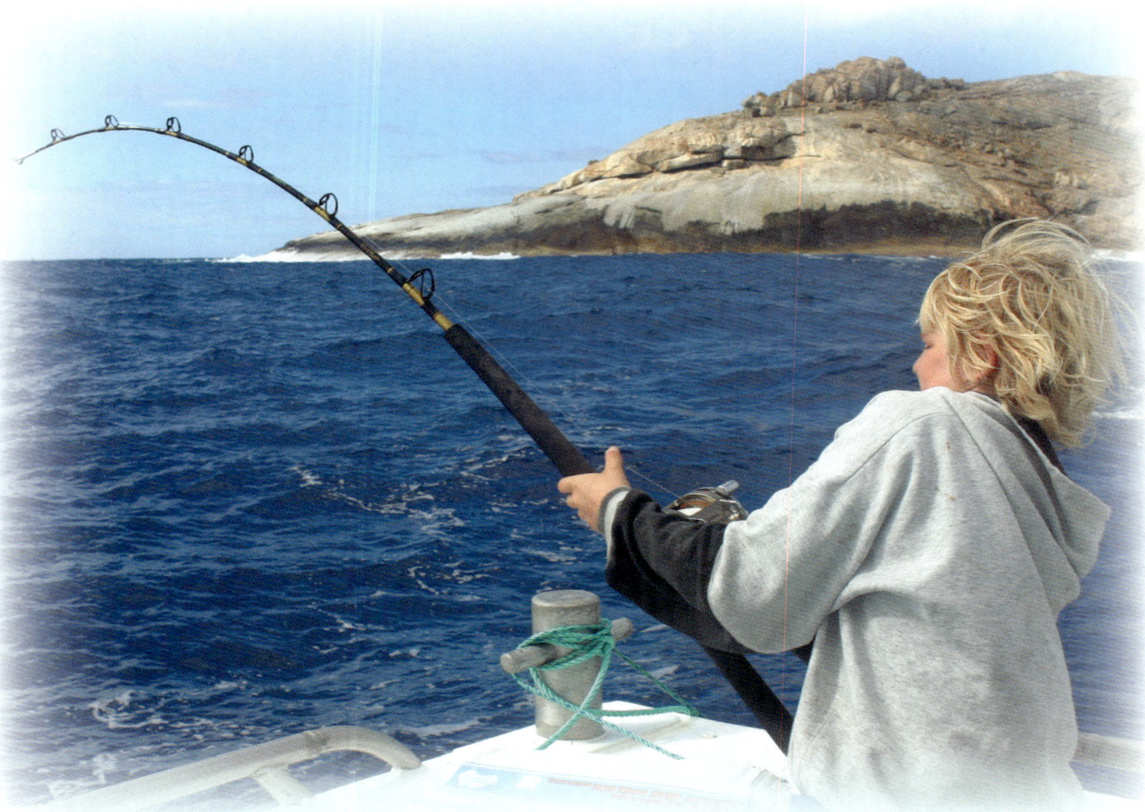

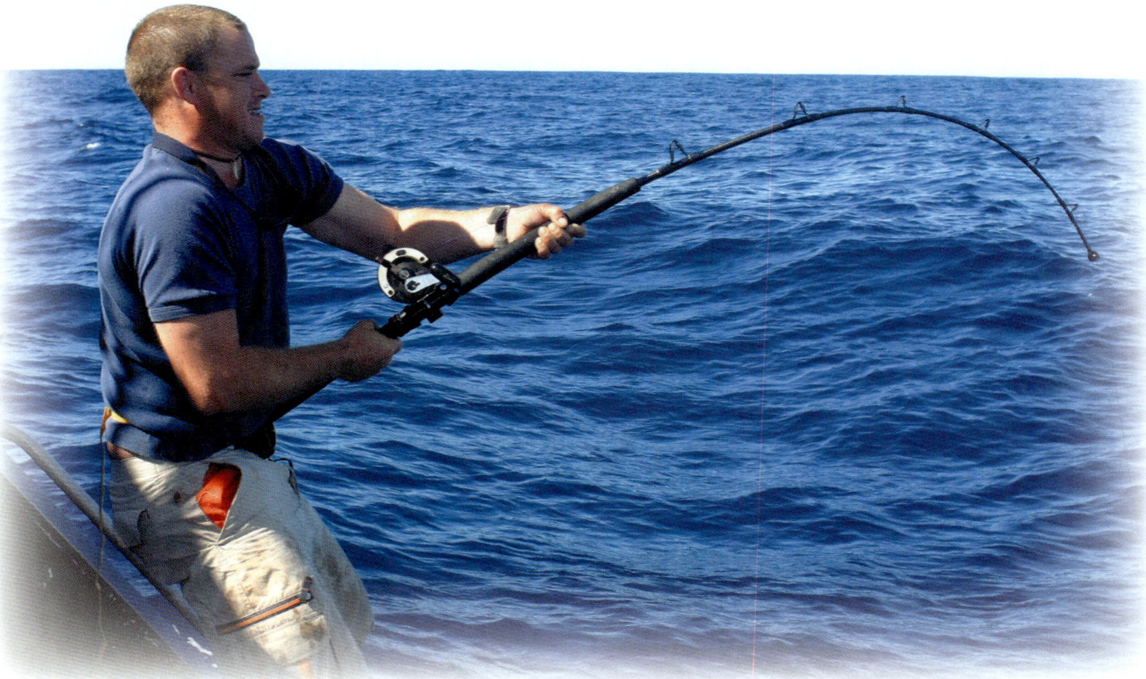

# INTRODUCTION

Bluewater sport and game fishing is one of the world's most popular forms of fishing. All sorts of anglers in all sorts of boats find excitement and challenge from the sea.

The boats that take the anglers to sea range from small tinnies through to mega dollar game boats and although the price of the boats may vary, they all have an equal chance at the fish.

The growth of trailer boats has seen an explosion in the number of vessels going to sea and, equally, the number of anglers enjoying their sport.

For some anglers blue water fishing may mean chasing billfish, big tuna or sharks, for others it may be yellowtail kingfish or mackerel while others may mix a bit of sportfishing with catching a few fish for the table, taking the best options available at the time.

There is room for a wide range of choices which is why many anglers find the game so fascinating.

There is also more to the sea than just fish. The sea changes everyday, sometimes calm and balmy and other times churned and violent. There are birds, seals, whales and the friendly dolphins, all add to the enjoyment and pleasure of being at sea.

The sea can be quite a place, something that absorbs, fascinates, challenges and rewards. The fishing is done on a backdrop of sky and ocean, providing something essential to our lives. Stories to tell, great excitement, times of real peace without high pressure distractions and often a fighting fish released or captured as superb food for our family and friends.

Those who go to sea understand the magnificent attraction, sometimes addiction, of the fish and fishing. This book aims to provide both the basic information and some of the finer points of bluewater angling to enable all anglers to get more from their sport.

It explains the various styles of angling, which once learnt can be used to catch fish anywhere. Learn the basics of fishing well and captures and fun will flow. Good fishing and gentle breezes.

Setting the lures as the sun rises over Kona, Hawii.

# CHAPTER 1

# THE BOAT

## THE FISHING VEHICLE

The boat is an essential part of bluewater fishing. It can make the fishing efficient and comfortable or it can make it frustratingly difficult.

Choosing the right boat and setting it up to fish effectively is an important part of enjoying offshore angling.

## SEAWORTHY

The first priority is for a seaworthy hull and a reliable engine. There are plenty of good boats around so take the time to get the purchase right.

Always look for plenty of work space, a clear, uncluttered stern area and good protection for the crew from the sea, wind and sun.

What usually happens is that anglers buy a boat, for whatever reason, and decide to make it go fishing. Some get everything right first go while many more get it right with their second purchase. This is why we suggest doing your homework before buying.

## BOAT FIT-OUT

Bluewater fishing boats will need some form of fit-out no matter what type of angling is undertaken.

The aim of the fit-out is to make the fishing as easy and efficient as possible. Some things are essential, some things are handy and some are just gadgets.

The following is a quick rundown on the bits and pieces and how they work. There are other books on the subject but some of the later fishing techniques described in this publication rely on the angler

Fast, modern vessels give anglers around the world access to good fishing.

understanding the correct boat set-up.

The real trick with getting the boat right is to fit everything in but leave the boat uncluttered so it works to help the angler.

RIGHT: Well engineered rod holders provide safe and secure positions for trolling rods.

BELOW RIGHT: Rod racks provide storage for gear not in use.

## ROD HOLDERS

Rod holders do a range of jobs. They store the rods while travelling and they secure them while trolling or setting baits.

Rod holders must be strong enough to hold the type of tackle being fished and an eye to the engineered strength of the rod holders is an important consideration, particularly when big fish are the target.

Rod holders are usually fitted with a small cross piece or pin in the bottom which secures the rod and reel in position, provided the rod is fitted with a matching gimbal at its base.

Rod holders are usually angled at 45° to provide both spread and a convenient fishing angle for setting baits and lures.

The end result should be that some rods angle out either side of the boat while some rods are set so they fish straight out the back of the boat.

This will provide a minimum lure spread of four lures on even the smallest bluewater boat and eight or ten possibilities on larger vessels.

It is essential that the rod holders hold the rods correctly so that when a big fish hooks up the line will run truly off the roller tip. On a rod holder which is not set square in the deck the line may end up running crookedly across the roller frame and cause a burn off.

## ROD STORAGE

Rod racks are often fitted to the cockpit area to help with rod storage. Overhead racks, called rocket launchers, are fitted to many vessels. These are mostly

ABOVE: Clean, simple layouts make fishing easy and trouble free.

BELOW: The bigger the boat the more you can do to it. Fly bridges and tuna towers add depth and range to your vision.

# THE BOAT

*Overhead rod storage keeps rods and reels out of the way and ready for use.*

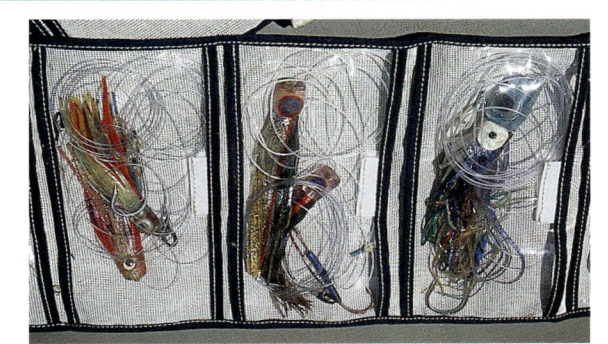

*Lure bags with clear acrylic pouches and washable rear fabric are a popular way to store trolling lures.*

used for rod storage but can also be used for trolling lures in certain situations.

Small boats always need some form of rod storage if more than half a dozen outfits are carried and while the problem is more apparent on small boats it can manifest itself on any size boat when lots of gear is on board.

## TACKLE STORAGE

Lures, hooks, sinkers and dozens of sundry items end up on fishing boats. Providing organised and dry storage is the key.

Good quality tackle boxes are best for hooks, sinkers and bits and pieces. Built-in storage bins and draws can help as can sealable plastic food boxes and bags. The important part is to carry only what is needed and used, the rest doesn't matter. Always try for neat, compact storage in any boat.

*Make the most of available space. This box mounts the seat, carries tackle boxes and holds a battery.*

## LURE BAGS

Storing trolling lures has always been a bit of an issue on most boats. Lure pouches and bags that wrap when stored or can be hung off a wall or bulkhead make a lot of sense.

These upholstered pouches are long wearing and reasonably priced. They use sewn, clear acrylic film so the lures can be easily seen and selected. They also keep the trace neatly rolled.

Many lure pouches also have breathable and washable backing fabric allowing the lures used during the day to be washed and dried with a minimum of fuss.

The same pouches are also used to store shark and marlin traces and help keep the boat neat and tidy.

When fishing starts they can be hung in the work area and make lure or rig changes quick and simple.

## LIVE BAIT TANK

This is an essential item in modern bluewater angling. The live bait tank uses water pumped through the storage box to keep the bait fish alive and available once on the fishing grounds.

The size of a live bait tank needs to be considered in most small boats as the weight of water carried can be considerable. The tank must be large enough for

*Live bait tanks are an essential part of modern sport fishing boats.*

the fish to swim around but not overly deep, with 25 cm (10 inches) of water depth being plenty so long as the tank has enough room.

Water is fed into the tank by a submersible bilge pump usually with a running water pick up fitted to provide water when the boat is running along on the plane. The exhaust water is piped or allowed to run overboard.

Prefabricated bait tanks are available from several manufacturers.

## BERLEY BUCKET

Berley buckets are used to pound fish, bread and other food items into a pulp which then drifts off to attract the target species.

Berley buckets are usually tubes with holes in the bottom and sides to allow the pulped mash to drift away. The mash is produced by a hand held chopper or just a piece of PVC tube that will break up the berley.

*Berley pots provide a clean and efficient method for attracting fish to the boat.*

It's important that the berley bucket sits immersed in the water when the boat is at rest. If it's just washed by wave action it will not work well.

## OUTRIGGERS

Outriggers are fibreglass or aluminium poles set in bases which allow them to be spread laterally when the boat is on the water.

Outriggers are used for both bait and lure trolling to provide spread and presentation. They also place the bait and lures outside the wake of the boat.

Outriggers, once spread, allow extra lures to be worked and give many lures an enhanced action by raising the towing point allowing the modern flat and cup faced lures more 'bite' on the water surface.

With lure trolling, tag lines are used to alter the towing point so there is little or no slack line between the rod and the lure so the fish is hooked on the strike.

Conversely, when trolling baits the outriggers and line holding clips can be used to provide an unweighted drop back so the fish can swallow the bait. A wide range of outrigger clips are available and these are designed to do a range of different jobs.

*Outriggers spread the width of the lure or bait pattern and add action and options when trolling.*

For most anglers a set of simple Pomponette clips, much like a heavy duty clothes peg, are as good as any and are basically foolproof.

Line release is usually provided by way of elastic bands of differing strengths depending on the job they have to do and the weight of the bait or lure being towed. On light lines some anglers use thin strips of chamois to hold the line in the outrigger clips without damaging the fragile nylon when a fish hooks up.

## DOWNRIGGERS

As the name suggests downriggers use large lead weights, known as bombs, to take baits and lures off the surface and down to pre-determined depths.

They add an extra dimension to trolling or drifting and present the baits down to 100 metres (300 feet) or more if necessary.

Boat speed effects the water drag on the downrigger weight, so the faster the vessel travels the shallower the lead bomb runs.

This has a marked effect when lure trolling at 8 knots, but still allows lures to run at 10 metres (30 feet) down.

At slower speeds, trolling rigged baits or live baits down deep can be deadly.

The slower speeds allow the lead ball to run easily to 30 metres (100 feet) or more when bait trolling.

It is an applied form of fishing where anglers can use the depth gained to present baits to fish working deep bait, hunting along a thermocline, moving around pinnacles or whatever.

It is up to the angler to incorporate the downriggers into their fishing pattern and apply techniques that will catch fish.

Commercial downriggers have been around for a long time and come in a wide range of designs, including electric drives and remote control units.

Most commercial units also have a depth gauge to show how deep the weights have been set.

Homemade downriggers are also easy to make using a deepwater winch or reel, strong rod and 100 kg (200 lb.) braid line. Depth markers are added by using small coloured bars on the braid at known intervals.

The heavy leads weights or 'bombs' are available at most tackle stores.

Like outriggers, downriggers can be fitted with a range of release clips for fishing with baits and lures.

Downriggers work and can be deadly at times.

## FISH STORAGE

The storage of fish for the table is an important consideration. Ready made ice boxes with padded lids can be built into the centre line of many craft and provide both a comfortable seat and a convenient place to store the fish.

Any fish kept for the table needs to be stored on ice. Many sport and game fish are spectacularly good eating and require an appropriately sized ice box and plenty of ice to keep them in prime condition.

*A big ice box is essential for handling large fish and keeping them fresh.*

## GAME CHAIRS

Game chairs are used to fight fish and they help anglers work heavy tackle more easily than stand-up angling.

While advances in rods and stand-up buckets and harnesses have helped many anglers fish heavier line classes, stand-up fights are not for everyone. Stand-up angling is far tougher physically than working from a chair.

*Game chairs take the weight of the tackle away from the angler and make the handling of big fish possible for everyone.*

Game chairs make catching big fish easy, because they take the weight of the tackle off the angler. For those learning the craft, young anglers, lady anglers and those of us who are not as fit or as strong as we once were a chair makes fighting game fish easy. The chair also helps those with bad backs or other physical disabilities.

The real issues on game chairs relates to the amount of space available on the boat and the amount of time to be spent chasing big fish.

If there is room and the boat chases big fish then a chair is well worth the money. The chair itself adds a couple of extra rod holders and the footrest is detachable on most models.

## SOUNDERS

Fish finders or echo sounders provide a two or three dimensional picture of the ocean floor and any fish between the ocean floor and the surface.

This information is depicted with either pixels

on a Liquid Crystal Display (LCD) or on a picture tube similar to a television picture tube.

The information can also be interpreted by the sounder, with features like bottom zoom to expand reef images or focus on particular depth settings like 10 or 20 metres (30 or 60 feet) above the bottom.

Sounders also have effective ranges, the depth to which they can fire a signal and receive it back at sufficient strength to give a good picture on the screen. This power is usually expressed in watts at a peak to peak (RMS) signal rate. The more watts fired through the transducer, generally the better the picture and the deeper the operating capacity of the sounder.

Like most electronic gadgets many sounders have a vast range of features which are virtually useless to anglers however they are often highly promoted by sales people.

The keys to look for when purchasing a sounder are power, screen quality, ease of operation, bottom zoom and if possible a built-in temperature gauge.

Do not buy a sounder that is difficult to operate, it will only cause frustration and annoyance. Stick with simple systems that make sense when you buy them. If in doubt ensure there is some on water instruction available before spending the money.

## TEMPERATURE GAUGE

As previously mentioned a temperature gauge showing the sea surface temperature can be a very useful tool. It is used to find particular bodies of water and can provide a range of clues to the likelihood or otherwise of fish being present in the area.

Having a gauge built into an echo sounder is handy but individual gauges can be fitted if necessary.

## GLOBAL POSITIONING SYSTEM (GPS)

Global Positioning Systems provide a relatively accurate latitude and longitude of a boats position on the face of the earth. This information is provided via a set of US military satellites.

While the GPS on its own provides valuable information its real benefit comes when combined with a screen and plotter which allows waypoints to be entered into the memory of the machine to mark reefs and places of interest. The actual GPS provides a great deal more information but it is the waypoints that are of most interest to anglers.

These waypoints are stored in the memory of the GPS and are available at the touch of a button. Having a large number of reefs and reference points in the machine allows the angler to move accurately from spot to spot or to find a favourite piece of reef without reference to landmarks.

Most GPS are relatively accurate but they are not absolutely deadly and this can vary depending on the availability of satellites to provide them with data.

The GPS system is being improved all the time and the use of differential GPS, a land located information source for the plotter makes the sets very accurate.

The cost of GPS ranges widely from cheap handheld units to large expensive television size units. As with most things electrical you tend to get what you pay for although any set with a plotter function will provide reasonable results.

The important thing to look for is screen/scale definition. Some screens come down to one nautical mile which is fairly inaccurate. More accurate GPS come down to one tenth of a nautical mile which is far more accurate.

Fishing electronics are improving all the time as the technology and its application is aided by developments in the overall electronic industry. As with many things in fishing, take the time to learn and understand the technology and its limitations before buying, it can save a lot of money. Properly used it will also help to catch a lot more fish.

## WORKING TOOLS

Every boat needs a set of stainless steel working tools to make fishing easier and more enjoyable.

Several companies produce stainless (no rust or low rust) hand tools specifically designed for anglers.

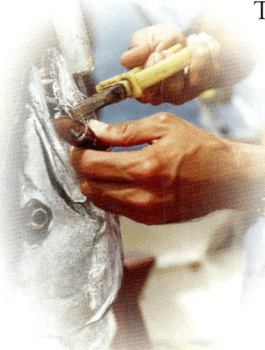

Hand tools are essential on every blue water boat. Take care when working fish with big teeth and bad attitudes.

These tools are often packaged in wearable pouches to keep them on your belt and within easy reach when fishing.

The main use of these tools is cutting line, trimming knots, cutting traces to release the fish, de-hooking fish and other bits and pieces.

The choice of tools is wide so it pays to buy the bits you need and then add more if necessary.

Some useful tools though are essential.

## LIGHTWEIGHT SIDE CUTTERS

These little nippers are extremely useful for trimming knots, cutting line and boat side releases.

They are sharp, light and cut accurately. They can usually work wire up to around 60 lb breaking strain.

## SIDE CUTTERS

Full strength side cutters are needed for working with heavy gauge wire and cutting hard surface materials.

They are also useful for nipping open the eye of fish hooks if ganged hooks are required and similar rough and tough jobs.

Side cutters are also needed to cut through hooks embedded in human flesh. It's never pleasant but it may be necessary.

## LONG NOSE PLIERS

A handy all round tool. The long nose pliers are excellent for removing hooks from toothy fish. Their cutting section will handle wire and heavy nylon and many come with a split ring opening facility built into the nose of the pliers.

This metal tooth allows for the ready changing of hooks and rings on minnow lures should they be damaged or bent.

Long nose pliers can also be used to 'tune' minnow lures so they swim correctly through the water.

## PLIERS

Standard pliers are useful on any boat as a general workhorse when fishing and in routine repair jobs.

Some of these tools also carry bits and pieces like bottle openers, wire strippers and all sorts of combinations. Their usefulness varies from plain gimmick through to inventive.

## BOLT CUTTERS

This might seem like a strange inclusion but bolt cutters are the only tool which will cut through forged game hooks and large chemically sharpened hooks.

Being a charter boat skipper your author has experienced the pain and horror of having large hooks driven through both his hands and arm. A few passengers have managed to do the same.

While an embedded hook alone can be managed, having a thrashing marlin or a wildly slapping dolphin fish (mahi mahi) on the same or joined hook can add an extra dimension to the suffering and physical damage done.

Decisive action and a pair of bolt cutters can remedy the situation quickly. Without the bolt cutters, there is little that can be done except hold on.

If there is a place to keep a pair of bolt cutters on the boat, carry them.

## KNIVES

Knives are tools of the trade for all anglers. They are an essential item for cutting line, preparing bait and cleaning the fish.

The important point with knives is to carry the right ones for the job. Much of this is personal preference but there are some knives that just work well.

Working knives need some rigidity and strength.

Knives are a tool of the trade, buy good quality and the right size for the jobs at hand.

A firmly bladed fillet knife is as good as any. A hard bladed knife is also useful for cutting berley and other bits and pieces.

For fish cleaning duties the knives must match the fish being handled. Big fish need big knives to handle the size of the beast involved.

A large boning knife is a good start and this can be used to quarter a big tuna and drop the fillets off the frame and then smaller knives can be used to produce the finished cuts.

This same large knife can cutlet a wahoo or mackerel or fillet a dolphin fish (mahi mahi). Smaller knives can then be used to produce cuts or fillets ready for the dinner table.

Knives are only ever as good as the person who uses and sharpens them. No knife stays sharp very long without attention to the blade. A sharpening stone or steel must be available to keep a good edge on a knife.

It does not take long to learn how to sharpen a knife. If in doubt ask your local butcher, fish monger or charter boat skipper to show you.

Having sharp tools makes fish cleaning and preparation for the table easy.

Most sport and game fish are remarkably good eating and some are exceptional on the table. If a fish is going to be kept for the table it is essential to have ice and storage to keep it in good condition and sharp knives to prepare it properly.

## CHARTER BOATS

The past decade has seen an enormous growth in the number of fishing charter boats operating around the world.

The charter boats cater to all tastes and between them offer a very wide range of fishing experiences. The fishing may vary a little depending on the location but most offer a range of vessels and fishing to suit the most common species in an area.

Many of the boats target reef fish or bottom fish while others may work on sport and game fishing.

Charter boats offer a very realistic and in many cases inexpensive way of going fishing. Watching a professional skipper and crew can also rapidly increase the skills and knowledge of an angler and anyone starting their fishing career should spend a few days on a charter boat to improve their fishing knowledge.

When you are the prospective charter boat customer a few points need to be checked before going to sea.

The first and most important point is whether the boat does the sort of fishing you are interested in. No point going reef fishing if you really want to go game and sport fishing. Always check this with the skipper. Agree on a price too.

The next steps will mostly come from experience and relate to the vessel and its gear.

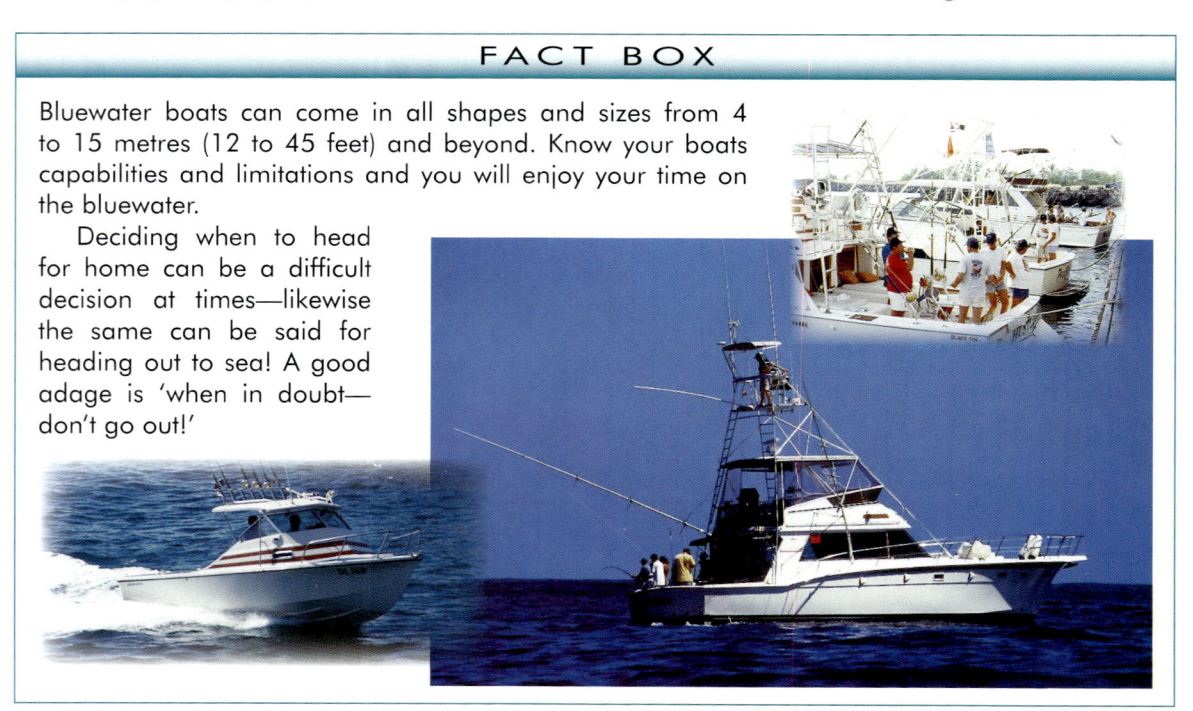

### FACT BOX

Bluewater boats can come in all shapes and sizes from 4 to 15 metres (12 to 45 feet) and beyond. Know your boats capabilities and limitations and you will enjoy your time on the bluewater.

Deciding when to head for home can be a difficult decision at times—likewise the same can be said for heading out to sea! A good adage is 'when in doubt—don't go out!'

*Modern charter boats provide a range of fishing options just choose the one that suits you.*

- check the boat is clean and tidy.
- does everything work—toilets etc.
- check if all the bait and tackle is supplied and if so it is in good operating condition and does it work well when the fish are hooked.
- is the skipper and crew helpful and willing to explain or teach.
- check on the disposal of the fish. This issue may vary from place to place.
- did you enjoy the day or the trip, if not find another boat.

The best way to enjoy sport and game fishing is to gather a small group of similarly interested anglers say four to six, and be able to book the whole boat. This usually leads to more enjoyable and productive trips.

Given the cost of buying and operating a bluewater vessel and our society's ever increasing demands on people's time, charter boat fishing can be expected to become more and more popular. With the right skipper and a group of friends it can be a very enjoyable way to spend a day or more at sea.

## SEASICKNESS

There is nothing better than a good day at sea but nothing worse than a day being seasick.

Seasickness is caused by a disruption of the fluid in the middle ear. This causes nausea and vomiting.

Different people react differently to its effects with some people coping and others being utterly stricken.

As charter skippers your authors have seen the full range of the dreaded 'mal de mere'. It can be controlled in most people but a few are destined to never overcome the condition.

Important points worth noting are:

- take anti seasickness pills at least one hour before departure.
- do not take ginger or quasi-natural remedies. From experience anglers might just as well eat the packaging as these useless pills.
- eat a normal, steady breakfast. Tea or coffee, cereal and/or toast are fine. Fried bacon and eggs and similar greasy foods are best avoided.
- a good nights sleep before going out is extremely important.
- avoid alcohol and big nights out prior to the trip.
- if seasickness does occur there is very little that can be done to help. However it is important to maintain body fluids so have a drink of water every hour or so.
- if you do get sick, the good news is that nobody ever died of seasickness no matter how bad you feel.

12    *Bluewater Fishing*

Medium sized marlin are best handled on overhead game reels.
PHOTO: DAVID ROCHE

# CHAPTER 2

# TACKLE

Bluewater fishing tackle is as diverse as the anglers who use it. Opportunities exist for using everything from trout gear through to magnum game reels and bent butt rods, depending on the fish species available.

The key to the tackle equation is choosing the right gear for the target species. This should allow the angler to fight the fish effectively and provide the level of sport desired by the angler.

The aim is to catch the fish and have some fun while doing it. For anglers who want to successfully catch fish the aim will always be to use realistic tackle for the job. Fishing extremely light gear and chasing rainbows is a matter of personal choice.

The trend to tag and release fishing has also changed the way many anglers fish. The aim now is to get the fish to the boat and release it while it is still strong and healthy. This means using tackle that matches the fish and can get the fish to the boat in a reasonable time.

This section on tackle concentrates on conventional angling, and while there are lots of options it tries to provide a middle ground for anglers of all standards.

## GAME REELS

There are two distinct types of game reels, those with star drags and those with lever drags. Both types though employ the revolving drum principle.

Star drags use a pressure disc system located on the main gear and drive shaft of the reel. The drag settings are produced by turning a star shaped threaded nut

*Star drag reels are great work horses and catch plenty of fish.*

located at the base of the reel handle which acts on a curved pressure washer pushing down on slipping plates housed inside the main drive gear.

Star drags use slipping washers that can only be as big as the inside area of the main drive gear housing. These are mostly about the size of a large coin. They provide a relatively small area for heat dispersion when big, fast fish are hooked.

Lever drags use a floating disc system that has drag washers basically the same size as the spool area. This large surface area allows for far greater heat dispersion from the drag washers when line is taken from the reel under pressure.

Because lever drags are not part of the drive system, it also allows for the fitting of free spool, strike and a wide variety of settings to be available at the angler's fingertip.

*Star drag reel in profile*

*Lever drag reel in profile*

A cutaway view shows the size of the drag and the engineering integrity in a lever drag reel.

It also allows for a preset strike setting to ensure the drag is applied at the right weight when the fish hooks up and the lever can't be pushed further forward by accident.

While both types of reels will catch fish, lever drags have a genuine advantage over star drag reels in most big fish situations.

It should be noted that some manufactures build their reels with genuine engineering integrity and some reels are built to a price. This is a fact of life but it is important for anglers starting out in the sport to learn the difference.

Anglers buying either lever drag reels or star drag reels need to look to the strength and performance of the reels they are buying. Asking experienced anglers and charter boat skippers will give a good guide to inexperienced anglers.

In general, the top quality lever drags make the best game reels but the quality star drag reels will still handle big fish without much fuss and at considerably cheaper prices. Just because a reel has a lever drag does not automatically make it a better reel.

Lever drag reels are designed for high performance fishing.

The proof of any reel is in its performance under great stress and its ability to last in a saltwater environment. Both of the above relate to the integrity of its design and the quality of its manufacture.

## THREADLINES

Probably the most versatile reel of all on a bluewater boat, threadlines can be used to fish lightly weighted baits, catch table fish off the bottom, cast, jig and troll lures, fish live baits for sportfish and work the lighter end of the billfish scene for sailfish and small marlin.

The key to threadline use on bluewater vessels is to only buy strongly made reels with premium drag systems.

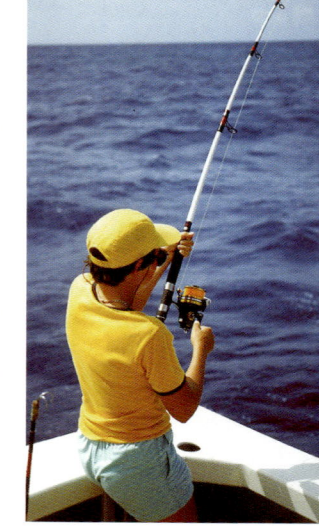

Technology has greatly advanced threadline reel performance with some threadlines now able to withstand drag settings and pressures that compare with high performance lever drag reels.

These reels have been specifically developed to match with braided lines and anglers chasing giant trevally (GT's), big yellowtail kingfish and samson fish. They will also handle billfish though their line capacity can be tested at times.

The reels are teamed with 20 to 40 kg (50 to 80 lb.) braid and used to cast or jig lures in heavy combat situations.

Modern threadlines can cope with tremendous pressure and big fish.

Naturally these reels are not cheap but they have elevated threadline technology by a serious margin.

Other useful additions on bluewater threadlines include a baitrunner type function which is most useful fishing for reef fish or casting unweighted baits for mahi mahi, yellowtail kingfish or small billfish.

The baitrunner allows the fish to take line under a controlled but very light tension. When the time to strike is right a turn of the handle engages the main drag, the angler sinks the hook and the fight is on.

Because casting is an essential element in using bluewater threadlines they need to be matched with light tipped rods for best results.

The rod needs a butt length of 30 to 40 cm (12 to 15 ins) to provide a comfortable leverage point while playing the fish.

Threadline reels are routinely used on small to medium billfish, they make for exciting fishing.

Light tackle overheads are used to catch a wide range of sport and game fish.

**Correct line loads for threadline reels.**

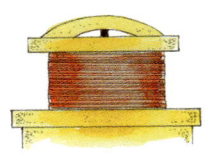

Under filled

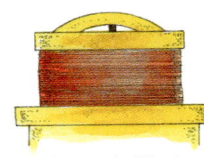

Correctly filled

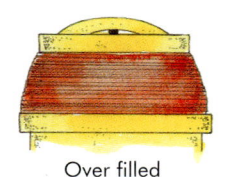

Over filled

Using short butted estuary type spinning rods will put tremendous strain on the wrists during protracted fights and these are not generally used in bluewater fishing.

Line breaking strains used are from 6 to 15 kg (12 to 30 lb.) depending on the size of the reel and the type of fishing being done. Braided lines up to 40 kg (80 lb.) are now appearing on some threadlines where magnum fish are the target.

Always remember that threadline reels only work effectively when the spool is fully topped with line. The reel needs the spool fully loaded to cast properly. The spool should also be kept full in case a big fish hooks up, when every centimetre of line may be needed.

Threadline reels are just so versatile and easy to use that they have become an essential part of the bluewater fishing scene.

## BAITCASTERS AND OVERHEADS

Baitcasting and other overhead casting reels are built using a revolving drum with gears and drag fitted to one side. This construction principle provides very strong reels with direct line contact to the fish.

Overhead reels and game reels work on the same principle but it is best to separate them for the purpose of this book.

Like threadlines, the small overheads are very versatile and can be used for bait fishing, lure casting, jigging, bottom fishing, trolling and live baiting.

They come in a wide range of sizes and are usually purchased with a particular role in mind. It is this role which determines the size of the reel needed.

Samson fish caught on a lightweight outfit.

The butt length of any overhead rod needs careful attention as it needs to be long enough for two handed casting and be comfortable when fighting the fish.

Shorter butts and shorter rods give good leverage against the fish but are not good for casting. Longer rods with longer butts give the best casting performance.

The best 'average' tends to be from about 1.6 to 2.0 metres (5' 8" to 6' 6") with a soft tip and plenty of strength in the lower two thirds of the rod.

When targeting tough bottom dwellers like yellowtail kingfish, cobia, cod, samson fish, amberjack, coral trout, emperor and sweetlips, a case for stronger rods can be made, it all depends on what the angler wants to do with the gear.

## ALVEYS

Alvey sidecast reels are extremely popular with rock, beach and estuary anglers as a no nonsense reel for inshore species.

RIGHT: Bottom fishermen and charter boat anglers often prefer the direct drive of the Alvey reels and winches for their fishing.

BELOW: Just to show their versatility the angler in the small boat fights a wildly leaping marlin on an Alvey reel.

Most baitcaster and some overheads are fitted with level wind devices which lay the line smoothly and evenly as the line is retrieved. On reels without this function the angler needs to lay the line with the thumb and forefinger during the retrieve. This may seem difficult at first, but rapidly becomes automatic once the angler becomes familiar with the reels.

Baitcasters tend to be used at the sporting end of the light tackle market particularly for trolling and lure casting.

Overheads tend to be able to work heavier lines and are used for everything from bottom bouncing and jigging to catching the larger sport and light game fish.

Again, the size overhead chosen is usually based on the general size of the target fish and their relative fighting characteristics or the overall use of the reel.

Overheads, as the name suggests, are fished on top of the rod and a couple of points about the rod are worth noting.

Rods used with an overhead reel should have the runners or guides spaced so the line runs from guide to guide and at no stage should the line touch the rod or go below the arc of the rod.

Many boat anglers use Alvey reels for close quarters bait fishing where light weight presentations are needed. Casting pilchards, garfish and other baits around the washes, floating strips and lightly weighted baits for reef fish and doing similar jobs, except lure casting, to threadlines.

Alveys need longer rods than most other boat rods to work well but in the right situation and in well trained hands they can be absolutely deadly.

For inshore anglers who work baits an Alvey should be a serious consideration. Even on bigger fish with heavier lines a large star drag Alvey can do a good job on fish like mackerel, yellowtail kingfish, mulloway, cobia and similar reef fish.

## WINCHES

Alvey has almost no competition for its deep sea winches and boat reels.

These winches are usually mounted to hand rails and are designed for working in deep water with heavy sinker weights. They are strong, well made and last a long time.

Smaller winches are also made for use on boat rods and these are common on many charter boats. Again, these reels are made to go straight up and down with heavy sinkers.

For anglers chasing reef and table fish winches are a very good answer. The only drawback is their weight, making them heavy after a few hours fishing.

## ELECTRIC REELS

As inshore reefs become more depleted and fish are harder to find there has been a trend to fish deeper and deeper reefs looking for quality table fish and larger sportsfish.

Winding any fish up from 100 or more metres (300 feet) of water can be a chore and some anglers simply cannot do it for an extended period. Handicapped anglers, older folk, kids, ladies and those who are not as fit as they could be all find deepwater fishing difficult.

Technology has the answer with electric reels.

These are overhead type reels that feature a 12 volt

Bottom fishing with electric reels is becoming more popular. They certainly save a lot of hard work.

Angler with electric reel and longfin perch.

drive system to retrieve both the fish and the line.

Most are duel system and the angler can wind the reel and fight the fish in the traditional manner or just switch the reel to electric drive and let the remote battery do all the work.

Having used these reels on our charter boat we can recommend them to anyone interested in deepwater bottom fishing.

Some of the more advanced reels even have jigging programs built into them so it is possible to jig yellowtail kingfish, samson fish, amberjack and other bits and pieces out in the deep without effort.

While these reels do not suit everyone they do have some advantages and they certainly make a hard job very easy.

They can also be a great help to many anglers who just want to enjoy the day and catch a feed of fish.

These reels will grow in use over time and they are fun and highly efficient fish catchers. They come in a wide range of sizes to suit all depth ranges and run all day on a small 12 volt rechargeable battery.

# RODS

Game rods are not made to do anything except fight fish and the way they are cut and tapered reflects this. They are also made to fish a line class or classes conforming with the rules of the International Game Fishing Association (IGFA).

The aim is to produce a rod which will pull a line to somewhere near its maximum breaking strain while providing an arc of leverage to lift the fish and cushion the line.

Some game rods are overly stiff for their stated breaking strains and while this may work well in highly skilled hands they are not very good at all for most anglers. Stiff unyielding rods can be just as hard on the angler as they are on the fish.

Rods up to 24 kg (50 lb.) should have tip movement in the top third of the rod. Even stand-up 37 and 60 kg (80 and 130 lb.) tackle must have some easy movement in the tip.

Rods built purely to work out of a game chair can be a little stiffer but we believe this offers few advantages to most anglers. The aim is to be able to work the fish comfortably and to enjoy the fight not endure a torture test.

When learning about game fishing, do not be afraid to overfish the rod by using one line class heavier than that stated on the rod. This will avoid break offs and once the experience needed to handle the fish is gained it is easy to change the outfits back to their stated line classes.

## GIMBAL

Starting at the bottom, a game rod, and many other bluewater rods, is fitted with a gimbal. This is a metal or plastic cross or key way and its job is to both keep the rod in place and to keep it straight when in a rod holder or being worked from a rod bucket or game chair.

## BUTT

The next section is the butt. This can be either straight or curved and long, intermediate, or short. It may sound confusing but the butt's length and shape indicate its use from a game chair or a standing position and both its length and shape influence the amount of leverage available to the angler. Game rods are all about leverage.

In general, longer butt lengths are used when the angler is working from a game chair. This applies to both straight and curved butts. The longer butt positions the reel so that it is at the right level to be wound and pumped from the chair.

The slightly longer rod is built so the rod tip goes out over the transom or sides of the boat and the line won't touch anything. With the angler basically stuck in the chair it is imperative that the rod can still work in close quarters situations.

Rods made to work with the angler standing have shorter butts, down to 30 to 35 cm (12 to 14 ins.), and are often called short strokers. The rods are shorter in length to give the angler greater leverage on the fish.

This type of rod was initially developed for tuna

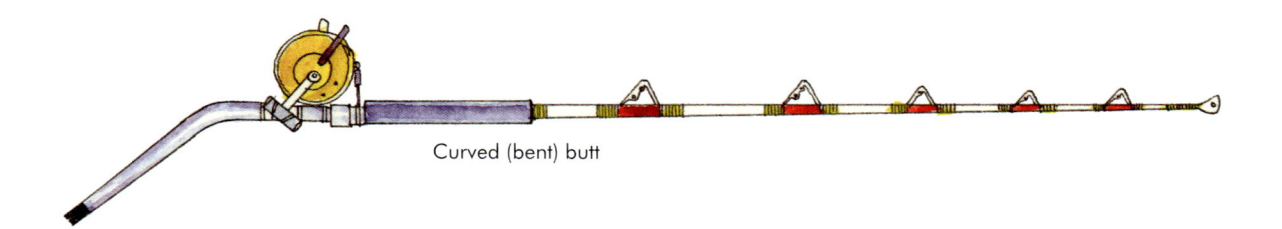

Three major types of game rods.

Stroker style

Straight butt

Curved (bent) butt

fishing and provides the power to lift big, tough fish out of the depths. Correspondingly, two speed reels were developed to give the angler more crank power through the reel in the same situations.

Intermediate butts are a compromise between the two extremes and are usually about 40 to 45 cm (16 to 18 ins.) from the butt to the centre of the reel seat.

Curved butts allow the angler to apply more weight and leverage to the fish for a given amount of effort. They are expensive but they do help, particularly on line classes from 24 kg (50 lb.) upwards.

## REEL SEAT

Reel seats on game reels are usually heavy duty with a thick collar to hold the feet of the reel. This is to hold the extreme forces that generate in this area during a fight.

To lock the reel into its correct place all game reels and most serious overhead reels are fitted with rod clamps. These are essential on game rods to anchor the reel firmly in position and keep it there.

Your authors have witnessed an angler who used his own gear on their charter boat including a 6/0 Special Senator on a stroker type rod, but failed to use the reel clamps.

When a big yellowfin tuna hooked up on a lure everything came tight fast and suddenly the reel flew out of the reel seat and slammed into the first runner where it stayed howling line off the drag for a few seconds before the line parted.

Luckily the reel was secured to a safety strap but the fish and the lure where lost. The foot of the reel showed how easily they can bend under heavy pressure when the rod clamps are not fitted.

## FOREGRIP

The foregrip on a rod is where a lot of the work is done pumping a fish. The foregrip must be comfortable and stay that way during long fights.

Some game rods are fitted with a long foregrip to provide extra reach and therefore extra leverage to the angler.

Beware of thick or fat foregrips. They might look smart but they can cause extreme cramping of the hands during a fight and are very difficult for young and female anglers to use with their smaller sized hands.

There are oval and triangular shaped grips which are meant to better suit the shape of the hand and in some cases they do but it is best to try them out first.

## RUNNERS

There are two basic choices of runners for game rods. One is the fixed ceramic ring type and the other is the roller guide. A case can be made for using either type of guide as both have plus and minus features.

Ceramic guides are low maintenance but have a higher rate of line wear than roller guides. Roller guides need a lot more maintenance and can be hard for novice anglers to keep straight during a fight.

One compromise which works well is a roller tip combined with ceramic guides.

On rods for seriously big fish and heavy tackle, where long fights can be expected rollers have a definite advantage. On small to medium fish, ceramics and a roller tip are probably the best choice.

Having said that also be careful of the quality of the guides fitted to rods. Like oils, runners ain't always good runners. Two rods can look similar but be priced $100 apart, most of this difference will be in the price and relative quality of the guides.

Where possible, Fuji ceramics and Aftco rollers are the best choice and clones of these vary from not bad to next to useless, so choose carefully.

## OTHER RODS

The previous section on reels has covered a little on rods but a few points need to be made.

As with almost everything in fishing there is no substitute for quality in fishing rods. This applies mostly to the hardware used to make them and the actual manufacture of the rods themselves.

Bluewater fishing involves real strains at times, this will test the tackle to its limits and low quality gear can be found wanting fairly easily.

For most situations the aim is to use gear that works well. If the rod is used for casting it must cast well, if it is used for bottom fishing it needs a sensitive tip to detect the bites and some strength in the mid-section for lifting fish off the bottom.

If the rod's function is right then the guides need to be smooth to prevent line wear and some cheap guides are not very smooth.

The other thing that can happen is the winch mount coming loose. This can and does happen, usually at the least opportune moment. It's caused by either poor packing or poor gluing during the construction of the rod.

Quality rods and reels provide the performance levels necessary to catch good fish together with the enjoyment of the fight without gear failure worry.

# FIGHTING GEAR

For a simple sport fishing certainly has a lot of accessories and bluewater fishing probably has more accessories than most sections of the game. But, the gear is needed and the angling system can't work without it.

## ROD BUCKETS

Rod buckets provide a secure spot to hold the end of the rod and protect the angler's stomach from bruising.

For bottom anglers, this can be as simple as a leather pouch the same as those used by beach and rock anglers. Once bigger fish come into the picture the actual protection provided by the rod bucket becomes serious.

Most rod buckets spread the load area across the lower stomach and top of the thighs and are made from solid materials with a foam backing.

These buckets also have a tube mounting to take the gimbal of the rod so everything locks tight when the pressure is on.

Manufacturers now produce coordinated harnesses and rod buckets to make standup fishing comfortable

## HARNESS

Harnesses come in several types. Most are based on a kidney design or a shoulder type but there are a few hybrids that use both waist and shoulder mountings.

Kidney harnesses are most useful when fighting in a chair or make stand up fights, particularly on tuna, more comfortable.

Shoulder harnesses are more general purpose and assist in a wide range of fights.

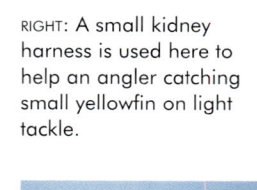

RIGHT: A small kidney harness is used here to help an angler catching small yellowfin on light tackle.

Hard wearing plastic rod buckets spread the load when fighting big fish.

LEFT: A shoulder harness is good for light tackle fishing but tends to put more weight on the lower back when using heavy gear

The trend to heavy tackle stand up fighting gear has also produced matching buckets and harnesses to enable the fight to be carried out satisfactorily. This gear needs the bucket low down on the anglers thighs and a combination type harness to work properly.

This sort of gear is purchased as a matched system of rod bucket and harness.

Always try the harness and bucket at the tackle shop before purchase to make sure it all works comfortably and you know how to hook it all up when the pressure is on.

## LANDING NETS

Landing nets are a handy tool on bluewater boats but they can get in the way on small boats where storage space is limited.

The best type has a big mouth and strong netting and can handle fish to 10 kg (20 lb) or more.

## GAFFS

Fixed gaffs are used on almost all fish except marlin and sharks. Most boats carry a 6 to 8 cm (2 to 3 ins) gape gaff for fish up to 20 kg (40 lb) and a 10 to 12 cm (4 to 5 ins) gape gaff for larger sportfish.

A little care needs to be taken with gaffing big yellowfin tuna as they can burst away with the gaff pulled from your hand and leave the crew looking fairly dopey. The fish then fights on with the gaff pole looking like a submarine's telescope as the fish circles the boat.

It sounds funny and it has happened to your author along with lots of other people who chase big

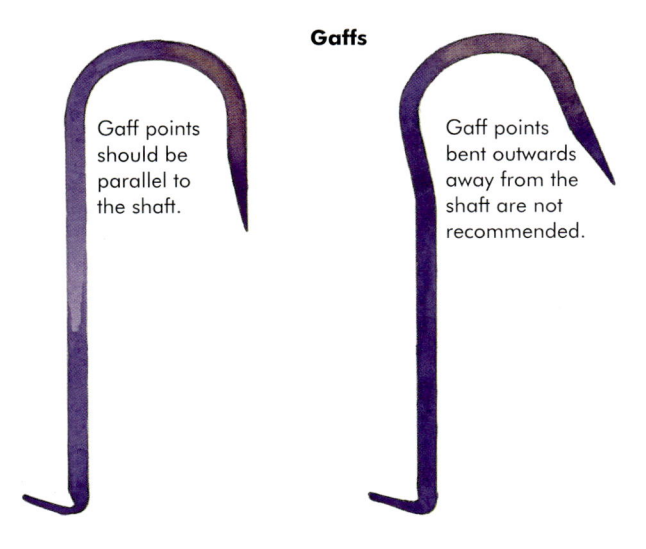

*Gaffs are an important part of fish landing, make sure you have the right tools for the job.*

**Gaffs**

Gaff points should be parallel to the shaft.

Gaff points bent outwards away from the shaft are not recommended.

tuna. Thankfully, most tuna are well beaten by the time they come to the gaff.

The only other sportfish to be wary of on the gaff are big cobia which can behave a bit like the sharks their body shape copies.

Marlin and sharks can both provide problems on the gaff and their thrashing and rolling means that flying head gaffs or wire lassos must be used.

On most vessels a 10 cm (4 ins) flyer is the workhorse and will handle fish up to 150 kg (300 lb) without problems so long as the steel in the gaff is up to the job.

For bigger fish and particularly bigger sharks a 15 to 20 cm (6 to 8 ins) gape gaff is the best choice.

Many anglers now use a wire lasso rather than a gaff and these have considerable merit as they can handle a wide range of fish sizes and do not rely on the bite of the gaff into flesh for their strength.

Gaff ropes should always be tied securely to a bollard as it is common for the fish to explode when the steel goes in and the only thing stopping it going anywhere is the gaff rope.

On sharks and marlin over 150 kg (300 lb) and particularly when they get up around the 250 kg (500 lb) size things can really cut loose on the gaff.

Small boats trying to land big fish should always consider putting a large foam buoy on the end of the gaff rope to avoid being pulled under or capsized by a big fish.

It's rare, but it can happen.

There are a couple of things to note when buying or making a gaff.

- always look for plenty of metal. Strong gaffs need enough steel in ratio to their size to work properly. Small, stout gaff hooks are always better than fine, wide gape models.
- all gaff points must be parallel to the gaff shaft or point slightly inwards like the point of a parrots beak.
- any gaff with the hook pointing outwards should be avoided. They are useless, difficult to land fish with and contribute to more lost fish than any other factor.

All gaffs should be kept clean and sharpened regularly with a file. A wipe with olive oil stops the rust getting in following sharpening.

## TAIL ROPES

Tail ropes are used to secure big fish after capture. They are usually a 2 metre (6 foot) length of silver rope with an eye spliced in one end and a tail splice at the other end.

The eye is passed under the tail of the fish and the tail end passed through it. Once this is done the rope is pulled tight on the wrist of the tail and the fish or shark is lashed flush against the bollard.

Once this is done the fight is over and everyone can relax.

Some anglers use a big stainless steel clip on the end of the rope and this also works well but it can be rough on the paint work if the fish plays up.

# HOOKS, SWIVELS AND SINKERS

## HOOK TERMINOLOGY

There can be no discussion on hooks without some knowledge of hook terminology. The diagram shows the basic parts of a hook. There are also a few terms that need understanding when talking about hooks.

RIGHT: **Parts of a hook.**

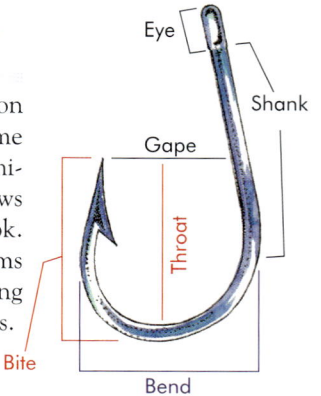

## Gauge

The gauge of the hook is the thickness of the metal used in its construction. This can be important from a strength point of view, its effect on shy fish or its ability to be driven into a fish on a particular line size.

## Temper

This reflects the relative strength, brittleness and suppleness of the metal in a hook. For example, the hooks used to make gangs of linked hooks need to be slightly softer in temper so the eye of each hook can be opened with sidecutters bent gently down and then closed around the next hook.

If the hook had a really hard temper like many of the chemically sharpened hooks they would just break if anything was done to open the eye or bend them.

## Forging

Forging flattens two sides of the round wire used as feed stock for nearly all hooks. Forging is like adding ribs to the steel. It makes the metal more rigid and stronger for a given thickness of metal.

## Pattern

This is the shape of the hook. Some patterns like Octopus, Viking, Long Shank, Limerick, Tarpon and so on are very well known.

## Kirb

The kirb or set of the hook applies to hooks that are bent crossways (offset) when viewed from above or below. The bending is done to improve the fish holding characteristics. The kirb can be to right or left and is indicated by being kirbed (right) or reversed (left).

Rather than try to explain every hook, we've developed a hook chart (*right*) that shows what we and others use most commonly on a range of fish or for rigging baits and lures.

It is a guide only and local techniques and styles will use particular hook types which work in that area. Personal preference is also a strong issue in any discussion on hooks.

## SHARPENING HOOKS

Most hooks straight from the box are relatively blunt and need sharpening with a file or stone. The

## HOOK SELECTION CHART

| Species/Activity | Hook Types | Size |
|---|---|---|
| **Bottom Fish/Temperate** | Viking/Octopus | 2/0 – 4/0 |
| **Bottom Fish/Tropical** | Viking/Octopus | 4/0 – 6/0 |
| **Yellowtail Kingfish/Live Bait** | Gamakatsu Live Bait<br>Mustad Hoodlum<br>Tuna Circle | 6/0 – 8/0<br>6/0 – 8/0<br>10/0 – 13/0 |
| **Yellowtail Kingfish/Dead Bait/Squid** | Octopus/Tuna Circle | 4/0 – 6/0 |
| **Mulloway** | Octopus<br>Tuna Circle | 4/0 – 6/0<br>10/0 – 13/0 |
| **Yellowfin Tuna/Live Baits** | Gamakatsu Live Bait<br>Mustad 9175<br>Mustad Hoodlum | 6/0 – 8/0<br>6/0 – 8/0<br>6/0 – 8/0 |
| **Yellowfin Tuna/Cubes/Dead Baits/Pilchards** | Tuna Circle<br>Mustad 9175<br>Gamakatsu Live Bait | 10/0 – 13/0<br>7/0<br>6/0 |
| **Lure Trolling/Marlin/Tuna/Wahoo etc.** | Mustad 7691S – 76LGS<br>Mustad 7731 or 7732S | 6/0 – 12/0<br>6/0 – 12/0 |
| **Marlin/Rigged Baits** | Tarpon (Needle eye)<br>Gamakatsu Live Bait<br>Mustad 7731 | 6/0 – 10/0<br>10/0<br>6/0 – 10/0 |
| **Marlin/Skip Baits** | Mustad 9175<br>Mustad 7731 | 8/0 – 10/0 |
| **Marlin/Live Baits** | Gamakatsu Live Baits<br>Mustad Hoodlum<br>Owner<br>Mustad 9175<br>Octopus<br>Tuna Circle | 8/0 – 10/0<br>8/0 – 10/0<br>8/0 – 10/0<br>8/0 – 10/0<br>8/0 – 10/0<br>13/0 – 15/0 |
| **Mackerel/Live Bait**<br>**Spotted**<br><br>**Spanish** | <br>Octopus<br>Gamakatsu Gangster<br>Octopus<br>Gamakatsu Gangster | <br>4/0<br>4/0<br>4/0 – 6/0<br>4/0 – 6/0 |
| **Cobia** | Octopus<br>Tuna Circle | 4/0 – 8/0<br>10/0 – 13/0 |
| **Trevally/Large** | Octopus | 6/0 – 8/0 |
| **Sharks** | Mustad Seamaster 7699 | 8/0 – 16/0 |
| **Dolphin Fish (mahi mahi)** | Viking<br>Octopus | 4/0 – 6/0<br>4/0 – 6/0 |
| **Garfish Rigged/Swim/Skipped** | Tarpon (Needle eye) | 6/0 – 8/0 |
| **Pilchards/Ganged Hooks** | Limerick<br>Gamakatsu Gangster | 4/0 – 5/0<br>4/0 – 5/0 |

exception is chemically sharpened hooks which are sharp and are actually degraded by attempts to sharpen them.

The best file to sharpen bluewater type hooks is an 8 inch Milled Bastard file. There are all sorts of other files and stones around and many work well. However, we are yet to find anything that can put a genuine point on a hook as well as a Milled Bastard.

## POINTS AND POINTS

There are quite a few different shaped points that can be sharpened onto a fish hook. The most reliable and easiest to produce is a three sided cutting edge point.

This is achieved by sliding the file down either side of the hook point with the file sliding slightly under the barb. When the point is sharp, the file is used down the top of the tip to make the tip finer and sharper.

The point is sharp yet strong and the finer sides will cut into tissue much like a hollow ground knife.

The system is simple, fast and effective and there is little need for anything more.

## CHEMICAL SHARPENING

Chemical sharpening produces vastly improved hook points compared to traditional milling and stamping of fish hooks.

A process using chemical baths produces both sharp and strong hook points.

This sharpening process has been applied to a wide variety of hooks, many of them used in sport, game and bottom fishing.

The only drawback of this process is that some hooks become highly reactive in saltwater and lose their points rapidly through the process of electrolysis.

Always check for this when using chemically sharpened hooks.

Not all makes suffer the problem but it is not uncommon either.

Some anglers treat the problem by wrapping thin zinc strips just under the eye of the hooks. This acts as a sacrificial anode and stops the hook point decaying.

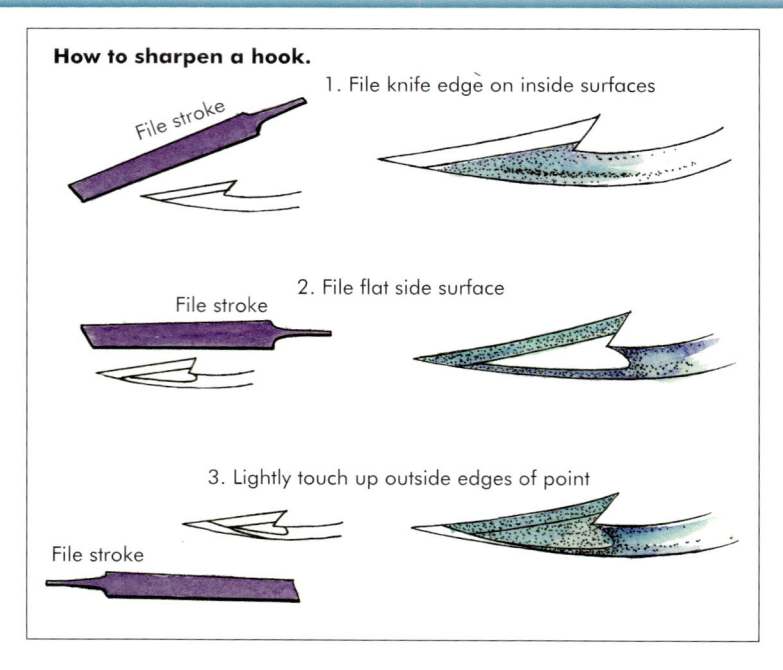

**How to sharpen a hook.**

1. File knife edge on inside surfaces
2. File flat side surface
3. Lightly touch up outside edges of point

## HOOK TECHNOLOGY

Keeping up with changes in hooks is a little like keeping up with fashions of any kind.

Some things come and go while quality and style remain forever.

All sorts of changes in fishing drives changes in fish hook design.

## TUNA CIRCLE HOOKS

Circle type hooks have gained very popular use with anglers because they are designed to lodge in the mouth of the fish. This eliminates gut hooking and provides healthy fish for tag and release. There are both fishing clubs and tournaments around the world where only circle hooks are allowed for bait fishing.

This is particularly important for anglers chasing billfish but they are also devastatingly effective on all sorts of fish.

The big issue has been that circle hooks were mostly made in commercial grades and strengths for long line fishing rather than lighter grades suitable for recreational anglers.

This situation has gradually been solved and there is now a wide range of circle hooks available in sizes and gauges relevant to anglers.

Many anglers find the circle hooks hard to use because of their shape but they are extremely effective. Using them will quickly bring confidence and this is important. There is nothing magical about circle hooks. They hook and hold fish very well but they also lose fish too. Nothing is certain in fishing.

The only trick when using circle hooks is to avoid striking. Slide the lever up to strike, let the weight of the fish come onto the rod and lean back.

Many anglers leave the rod in the rod holder and just slide the drag lever to strike and allow the fish to hook itself.

Once hooked, fish find it very difficult to dislodge circle hooks.

## STRONGER, FINER

For many years Mustad 7691S have been the mainstay of the lure trollers around the world.

The demands of anglers for lighter hooks and finer gauges has lead to Mustad developing the 76LGS. It is the same hook just a lighter, finer version more suited to light tackle and active lures.

On the same subject there are also some very powerful, lure related hooks coming out of Asia. These hooks tend to be more curved than the Mustad patterns but they have great fish holding characteristics.

Their big drawback is that many are not stainless steel and have a limited life in saltwater.

## BRAID

The trend to using braid lines combined with tough tackle and heavy drag settings has had a big impact on hooks. Many anglers rapidly find out that the direct contact, no stretch of braid plus big, strong fish finds its weakest link at the hook.

Braid lines open out a lot of hooks. When using braid lines always use premium, high strength hooks.

## SWIVELS

Swivels are designed to remove or minimise the amount of twist in fishing lines. They also act as a strong and convenient method of joining fishing lines to traces.

The key to using swivels in bluewater sport and game fishing is to choose the right size and strength for the job being done.

Budget style swivels may be good for bottom fishing and light tackle trolling but they can be found wanting in serious fishing when real pressure is exerted by both the fish and the angler. Ball bearing swivels generally provide the best results for game and sport fishing.

For heavy duty fishing, pay the money and buy quality.

## SNAP SWIVELS

Snap swivels are the main link point in most game fishing rigs and they tend to get a lot of work particularly when trolling lures.

In most game fishing situations it is rare to lose a snap swivel so it's possible for a swivel to stay in place from season to season. Even the best quality swivels don't last and it is a good idea to change to new ones each season.

As with ordinary swivels, always buy top quality snap swivels as the strength of some of the cheaper models can be suspect.

Some of the snaps or clips on some swivels also 'trip' and lock out of shape when trolling. Any swivel that does this is going to be a problem when a fish hooks up.

There are several different types of snaps or clips and anglers can make their own choices on these. The two main types used are Coastlock and McMahon Snap (Hawaiian Snap).

Both work and it is mostly a matter of personal choice which swivel is used.

## RINGS

Mostly made from solid brass or stainless steel these tough little rings are used as connectors for all manner of traces.

## SINKERS

Sinkers are a necessary part of almost all bait fishing and bait rigging. The main sinkers used in bottom fishing are Snapper or bomb types. Various sizes of these are used from 30 grams (1 oz) to 500 grams (1 lb) and even 1 kilogram (2 lb) in very deep water.

Ball and Bean sinkers are used for lightly weighted rigs and large 250 to 500 gram (½ to 1 lb) Barrel sinkers are used for deepwater live bait rigs for yellowtail kingfish, mulloway and cobia.

Ball and Bean sinkers from 30 to 90 grams (1 to 3 oz) are used in bait rigging for producing swimming baits.

Small Split Shot are used on handlines for bait catching.

Most anglers seem to carry far more lead than they need, it's part of fishing. The important part is to carry the lead that is needed for the job at hand.

# LINES

Fishing lines are the very heart of the angling system, they are the link between us and the fish and they need careful consideration to get best results.

## MONOFILAMENT

Monofilament or nylon lines have been the mainstay of angling for the past half a century. They are being superceded by braided lines in many forms of fishing but they still have a very important role to play.

Monofilament is a form of extruded nylon and a variety of formulas can be used to give the line a particular set of characteristics.

Some of these include the amount of stretch in the line (all monos stretch), its diameter for breaking strain, its abrasion resistance, its level of polish, uniformity of thickness and its suppleness or softness. Some nylon lines also have a 'memory'. This is a retention of the coils they are laid into when placed on a spool. Lines with memory are not easy to use and are best avoided.

The important choice with monofilament lines is to get the balance of required features for each job.

A threadline reel needs thin diameter line for breaking strain because threadlines lack big spool capacity. The line also needs to be supple to work light baits and sit well on the spool.

Games reels work best with lines that have limited stretch. This is important when fish take a trolled lure and when trying to lift tough fish from the deep. They have average or even large diameter to minimise surface wear and very good knot strength.

Monofilament tracing systems make rigging easy. The trace can clearly be seen on this tagged striped marlin about to be released.

Most of the 'learned' knowledge with monofilament lines comes from using it out on the water. Anglers can then pick and choose what works best for them and their fishing technique.

As with most products, quality brands will state and provide the sort of features needed for various types of angling.

## BRAIDED LINES

Braided or fused lines are made from multiple strands woven together to form a single thread. They are far more expensive than nylon lines and offer both advantages and disadvantages.

Braided lines have far less diameter than monofilament lines of the same breaking strain. Braided lines also have little or no stretch.

The major application for braided lines includes bottom fishing, casting lures, jigging and deep water fishing of all kinds.

Working with reef brawlers like yellowtail kingfish, amberjack, trevally, grouper and cod suits braided lines.

Trolling for big game fish with braided lines has its limitations. Do not mix trolling gear where some outfits have braid and some have mono.

When fish hook up the braid will cut the mono very easily if the lines cross or even touch under pressure.

The braid also transmits a lot of movement and 'shock' back to the angler, particularly on big, jumping fish like marlin.

Conversely, shark anglers can use the lack of stretch in braid to lift stubborn beasties out of the depths.

It is all a matter of applying the right tools to the job when deciding to use nylon or braid. Each line has a role to play, it just depends on the circumstances.

It should also be noted that braid type lines generally do not meet line class classifications provided by IGFA. If you are fishing for records or in tournaments it may be necessary to fish with monofilament lines.

## NYLON TRACE SYSTEMS

Making nylon traces and rigs using metal sleeves or crimps is an important part of modern bluewater sport and game fishing.

Almost all traces for billfish and larger type fish are made on crimped nylon tracing systems, as are most trolling lure rigs.

**Rigging and crimping nylon traces.**

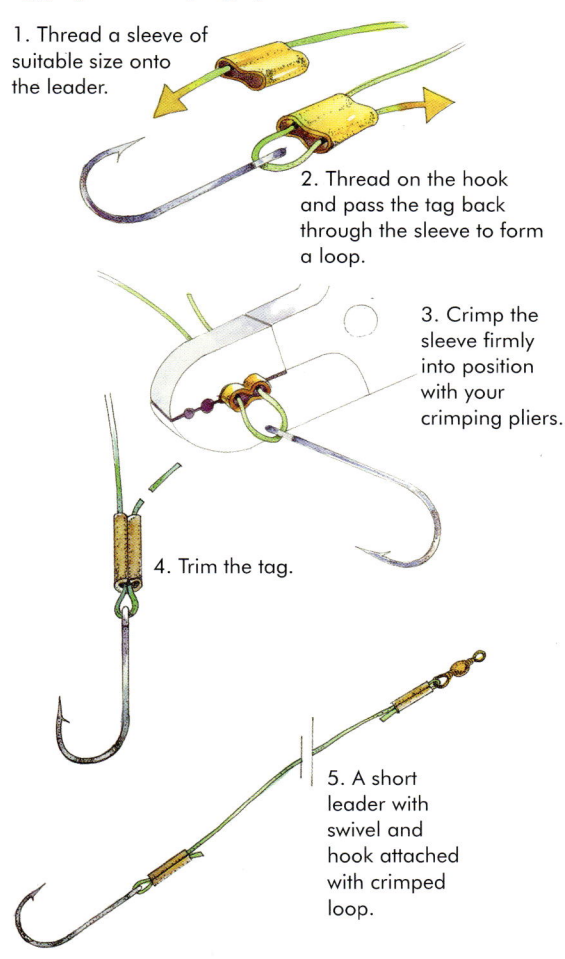

1. Thread a sleeve of suitable size onto the leader.

2. Thread on the hook and pass the tag back through the sleeve to form a loop.

3. Crimp the sleeve firmly into position with your crimping pliers.

4. Trim the tag.

5. A short leader with swivel and hook attached with crimped loop.

There are several makes of trace available with Jinkai probably the best known followed by Hi-Seas, Tortue and Sure Catch.

The trace material comes in all sorts of thicknesses to meet angling demands and the different needs for traces.

In fact trace and sleeve combinations can now be purchased down to as small as 10 kg (20 lb) for estuary and freshwater applications. At the other end of the spectrum nylon traces can be purchased up to 500 kg (1000 lb) breaking strain.

The common breaking strains used are 50 kg (100 lb) for yellowfin tuna on bait, 75 to 200 kg (150 to 400 lb) line for marlin and bait trolling rigs and 100 to 300 kg (200 to 600 lb) for lure trolling rigs. The size trace being used relates to the size of the fish being chased or expected and the size tackle being used.

To make the tracing system work needs more than just nylon trace. Crimping tools that compress the crimps and sandwich the mono rather than slam them shut like wire sleeves are needed. Plastic and metal thimbles to protect the line in high wear contact areas and wire coils and plastic sheaths for similar jobs are all part of the system.

The essential items are the crimps, pliers and thimbles for most small boat rigs. The other bits and pieces are essential for heavy tackle angling.

When making traces for bait fishing, the mono is crimped at the eye of the hook at one end and around a brass ring or swivel at the other. We don't use any protective material on the trace nor do we use a Flemish Eye which is really a wire tie and should not be necessary when using nylon line.

The same applies when rigging baits for trolling, just crimp on the ring for attaching to the swivel and run the nylon through the head of the bait, add a sinker if necessary and close the crimp.

On trolling lures a plastic thimble is used on the end connecting to the solid brass ring and a metal thimble to connect to the stainless shackle which holds the hook and second hook to the trace. These thimbles are designed to minimise wear and protect the trace.

This works fine on gear to 24 kg (50 lb). On heavier tackle, metal thimbles at both ends of the trace can be used, or a plastic sheath can go over the trace before crimping. The thimbles or sheaths stop any line wear or fatigue in high pressure areas.

The key to the system is to buy the leader in the sizes needed, thimbles, matching crimps and crimping pliers so the whole system goes together easily.

This system is indispensable on any bluewater boat. It is easy to use and provides a very secure method of making traces.

## WIND-ON LEADERS

Wind-on leaders are designed to allow anglers to wind their fish very close to the boat to enable tagging or gaffing without handling the trace or physically tracing the fish.

A piece of woven dacron is opened to form a tube and the line and trace are drawn inside this tube from either end.

The surface area of the woven tube holds the line tight and this enables anglers to wind the trace through the runners and onto the reel.

On made up rigs such as trolling lures or shark traces the rigs are made shorter, about 1 metre (3 feet) or a little more and they are then clipped on the end of the wind-on by a snap swivel.

Wind-on traces can be purchased in ready made form or anglers can make their own, it depends on personal choice.

## COMBINATION TRACE SYSTEMS

Nylon coated wire can be joined to nylon trace material to produce combination traces. These have a range of uses.

Some anglers add on a 30 cm (12 ins) piece of 150 lb nylon coated wire to their marlin skip or drift baits to handle pesky but sometimes wanted hammerhead, mako or whaler sharks.

It is also used to join a short length of wire inside skirted lures to provide the low visibility of mono in front of the lure with the toothy critter protection of wire inside the skirt of the lure.

Combination traces are produced by using an over size Hi-Seas (ribbed) crimp and then threading the mono trace in one side and the nylon coated wire the other. The tag ends are then folded back into the crimp and pulled flush to the edge of the crimp. The crimp is then firmly closed with the pliers and the nylon and wire are joined.

Alternatively, plastic coated wire can be tied direct to the line using an Albright Special knot although the connection of the wire to a hook should be done with a crimp.

**Making a combination trace**

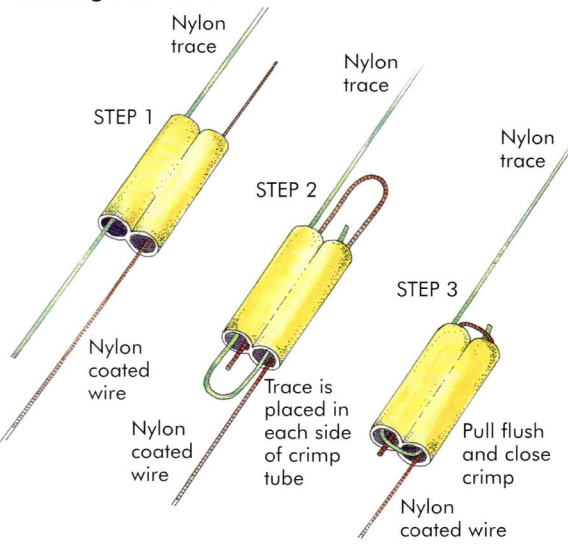

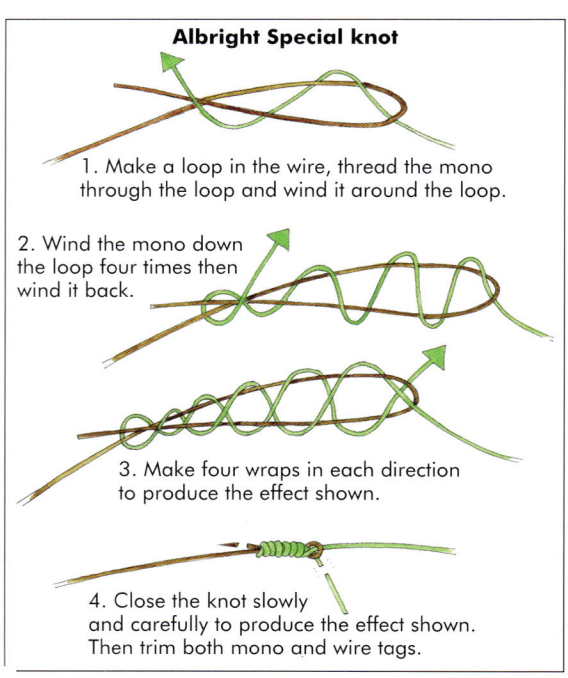

STEP 1 — Nylon trace / Nylon coated wire
STEP 2 — Nylon trace / Trace is placed in each side of crimp tube / Nylon coated wire
STEP 3 — Nylon trace / Pull flush and close crimp / Nylon coated wire

**Albright Special knot**

1. Make a loop in the wire, thread the mono through the loop and wind it around the loop.
2. Wind the mono down the loop four times then wind it back.
3. Make four wraps in each direction to produce the effect shown.
4. Close the knot slowly and carefully to produce the effect shown. Then trim both mono and wire tags.

# WORKING WITH WIRE

Wire is an essential part of many fishing systems. Modern skirted trolling lures, shark anglers, anyone chasing mackerel or wahoo and some big marlin anglers all use wire one way or another.

Wire comes in several different forms and understanding how these work makes fishing with them easier.

## SINGLE STRAND WIRE

This wire, as its name suggests, is made of one solid strand. It comes in a few grades of hardness but only one is of real value. This is the hard drawn, pre-straightened wire sold in either galvanised or brown colour. Most anglers choose the brown wire.

This wire comes in a wide range of breaking strains or in wire parlance its diameter size in millimetres.

For most anglers, the sizes worth worrying about are as follows:

- 014 or 40 lb wire is used for traces for spotted or Spanish mackerel. Where Spanish mackerel are large or common .016 or 60 lb wire is used.
- Light tackle marlin anglers who rig troll baits with wire generally favour .022 for line classes up to 15 kg (30 lb) and .024 for 24 kg (50 lb). Bait trollers rigging mullet, slimy mackerel and garfish for mackerel and wahoo use the same size wire.
- Anglers fishing for big marlin on wire and 37 kg (80 lb) or 60 kg (130 lb) tackle generally use .036 wire. Some big shark anglers also carry a few single

## Rigging with a single strand wire.

1. Thread on your hook o swivel and make a loop ir the wire, holding the tag and main strand apart wit thumb and finger. Then rotate the loop so that a twist forms. Complete 5–7 twists. Then bend the tag back over the twists so the the last twist becomes a sharp right angle bend.

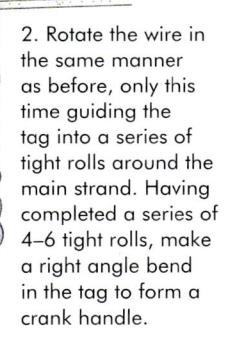

2. Rotate the wire in the same manner as before, only this time guiding the tag into a series of tight rolls around the main strand. Having completed a series of 4–6 tight rolls, make a right angle bend in the tag to form a crank handle.

3. Using the crank handle, rotate the tag in the opposite direction to your rolls and this will cause the tag to snap off.

## Rigging with multi-strand wire.

1. First select a sleeve of the appropriate size and thread it onto the wire. Tie a simple overhand knot in the wire, threading the tag back through the eye.

2. Add an extra wrap to the knot.

3. Thread the tag through the sleeve.

4. Work the knot down onto the eye as small as you can and crimp the sleeve down really hard on the wire with a pair of crimping pliers. Then cut the tag off as close to the crimped sleeve as possible.

strand rigs for cagey whalers and hammerheads that shy off conventional traces.

❖ Single strand wire is tied with a Haywire Twist and Barrel Roll combination. This tie takes a little practice but is relatively simple to produce.

## SEVEN STRAND WIRE

Seven Strand wire as the name suggests is a multi-strand wire which is supple but retains some rigidity though it can be distorted and bent fairly easily.

It is a general purpose wire and is used as trace material (brown) for mackerel fishing and in larger sizes for shark fishing.

The wire is joined to terminal tackle by way of crimps although it can be tied to hooks and swivels using a blood knot in its smaller sizes. This wire is also sold in a plastic coated form.

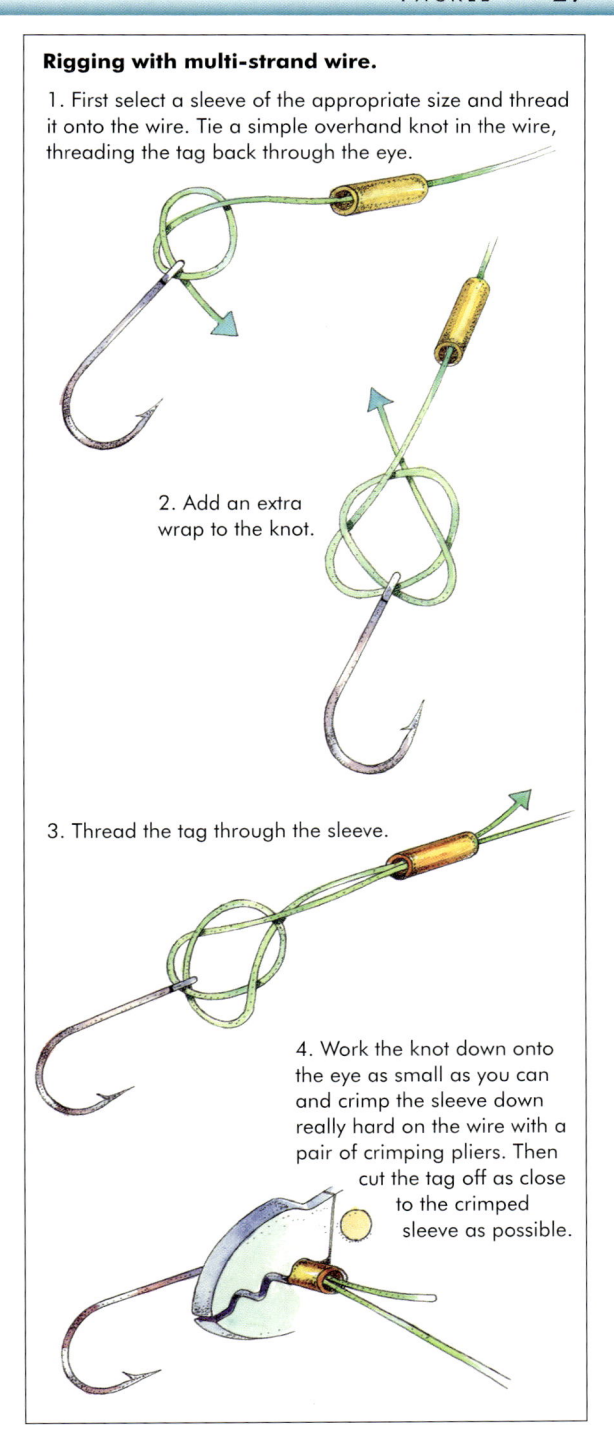

## 49 STRAND WIRE

This woven multi-strand wire is very soft and supple and is ideal for shark fishing. It can be bitten off occasionally by big makos and whites but in general it makes an excellent shark trace.

For most small sharks, 125 kg (250 lb) 49 strand is a good standard with heavier wire used for larger sharks.

## CABLE WIRE

High strength stainless steel cable wire is used to make both shark traces and the short traces used for the second hooks on skirted trolling lures.

Most of the cable wire used for lures is around 300 kg (600 lb).

For shark fishing, cable traces are mostly used for very large sharks although aircraft grade cable like Bowden Cable can be used for most large sharks. Some cable wires also come plastic coated.

## WIRE TIES

Single strand wire is tied with a Haywire Twist and Barrel Roll combination. This tie does take a little practice but is relatively simple to produce.

When using any of the multi-strand wires, a loop called a Flemish Eye is formed to spread the weight loading around the wire rather than concentrating it all in one place.

If the wire were crimped in a simple loop it will still hold quite well but under strong pressure the wire can be bent over the snap swivel or hook eye hard enough for it to break. Wire does not like to be bent or kinked and it will work harden and break once it is firmly kinked. With the Flemish Eye formed, the trace is crimped firmly into place.

## PLASTIC COATING

While many different wires come with plastic coating be aware that rust spots can form inside the coating and eat out the wire. Where possible always check the wire for rust which is usually easy to see.

Where wire is an essential part of the fishing scene,

---

### FACT BOX

# LINE CARE

Line care is an essential part of bluewater fishing. Everything hinges on that taut piece of nylon staying together once the hook goes in.

Anglers need to be very conscious of factors that can cause damage or wear to the line.

Simple injury to the line can occur in day to day fishing. Real abrasion will be felt as it passes through the fingers. Any abraded line should be removed immediately.

More sinister damage happens with things like lure crossovers, when one line may wrap around another line many times. If one of the lures is imparting a lot of weight to the line, like a big minnow does, pulling hard to try and sort out the crossover will cause friction damage to the line under stress.

To avoid this problem, any crossovers should be wound to the boat using both rods, retrieving at the same pace so that no undue stress is placed on either line.

Multiple hook ups can also result in crossed lines or lines running onto or over each other. This will also cause line damage.

Just as an item of interest, when heavy line and light lines cross and both have fish on, the light line will almost always cut the heavy line.

It's just a matter of physics, both lines will be damaged.

The only way to avoid a cut off is for both or all anglers involved in the crossover to go into either minimal drag or hand controlled free spool until the knitting can be unpicked and everyone is free to resume fighting their fish.

Just remember when the fight restarts that it is almost certain that one or all of the lines involved will be damaged so anglers should fight the fish firmly but gently until the point where the crossover occurred is back on the reel.

Whenever incidents happen during a fishing day that involve line damage, the results should be checked either on the return to shore or actually on shore to ensure no damage has occurred or replace any lines that have been damaged.

The same goes for line involved in long battles or in repeated battles with big fish. Line wear is real particularly on fixed guides but also on rollers. Any line exposed to more than four hours fighting time on fixed guides and six hours on rollers should be changed for new line.

Hooked up. The right result after finding the fish.

take the time to learn a little about its characteristics and have sharp pliers or side cutters to work it easily. Always use the right size and type of crimps for the wire.

When rigging for toothy but sometimes bite shy fish like mackerel, wahoo or dogtooth tuna always use wire that is strong enough so the fish can't bite through too often, but light enough so they will still hit the bait.

**Rigging with heat welded multi-strand wire.**

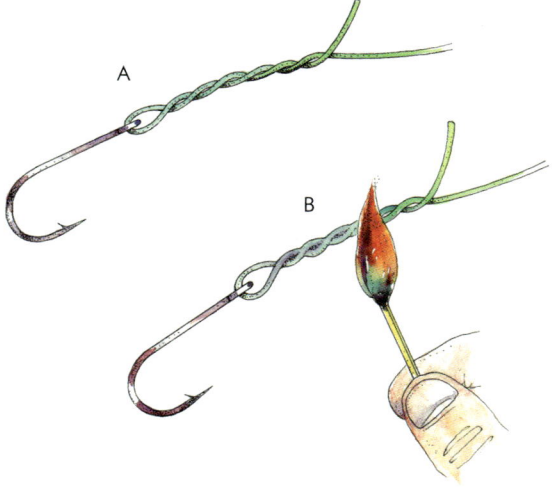

## HEAT WELD WIRE

Heat welded wire is an easy and useful system to use for many light game toothy species. It is very easy to use, simply produce a Barrel Roll and weld the roll with the heat from a match or cigarette lighter.

Game boats with a fly bridge are an advantage for a crew looking for game fish.
PHOTO: BILL CLASSON

# CHAPTER 3

# FINDING FISH

Many people regard the sea surface as featureless, blue and barren, just water and more water. To an angler though the sea surface means everything for it is here that the signposts for finding the fish are located.

## WATER COLOUR

Seawater comes in a variety of colours. Inshore water is often many shades of green, during floods it may be muddy brown, sometimes the offshore bluewater current pushes right to the coast and it too has many shades.

Whatever the reasons, water colour does have an effect on many oceanic fish. Learning to relate this to the fish does help with captures.

Much of this relates to experience and some of it is just supposition but water colour is important.

## Green Water

Inshore water is usually green but relatively clear and both inshore fish and larger game fish will feed in green water. However, green water which is also cloudy can be a very poor fish producer.

Often where green water and blue water meet is highly productive for game fish.

## Blue Water

Genuine oceanic water is always a deep blue colour, sometimes it is intensely so with a deep cobalt hue and even the outboard bubbles have a light blue rather than white appearance.

This type of water is favoured by most anglers chasing offshore game fish.

Various shades of blue also appear and these effect catches to some degree although it is hard to be definitive about it.

Real bluewater can be the deepest shade of cobalt. Check the outboard bubbles for a great colour tone compared to the white of the surface splash from a small black marlin.

## Crystal Clear

Absolutely clear water may be good for scuba divers but it makes for generally terrible fishing. Clear water is clear because it is devoid of plankton and other marine life and with no plankton for the bait fish there are no bait fish and no bait fish means no bigger fish and so on.

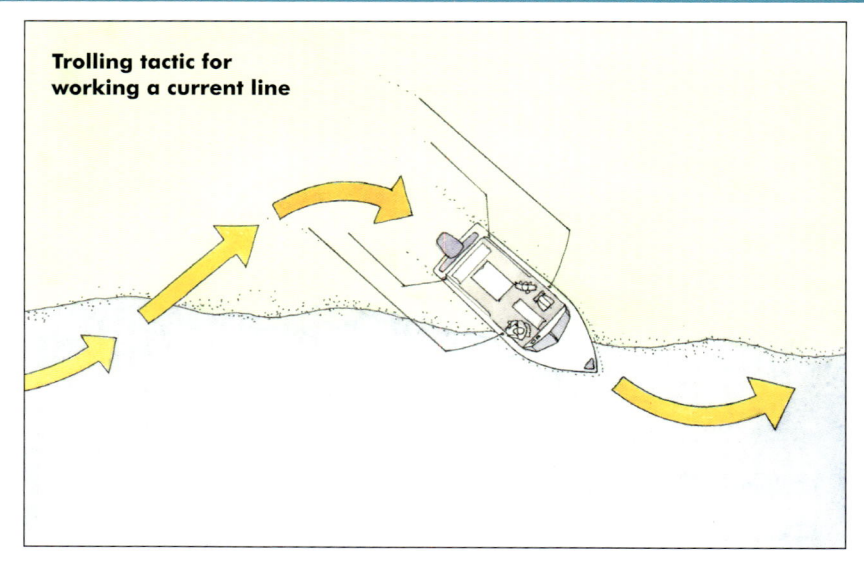

## Black Water

Usually caused by cold water rising to the surface, black water is not good fishing water although some cold water species like salmon, barracouta and yellowtail kingfish will bite in it. Game fish seem to give it a big miss.

Always take note of the water colour as it does have some bearing on the fishing every day.

**Trolling tactic for working a current line**

RIGHT: Solid current lines where dirty water meets bluewater are always likely spots for big fish.

## CURRENT LINES

The sea is not a static place, water moves great distances in both swirling currents and with the tides.

Often these moving bodies of water run into each other causing highly visible current lines. These can be very subtle colour changes or they can be marked lines of confrontation as the water boils together.

Sometimes the lines are marked by flotsam and jetsam with weed and modern garbage marking the line.

Whatever the reason, current lines are also patrolled by game fish and sharks like a boundary rider cruising a fence. These places are always likely to hold good fish and trolling baits or lures or drifting and berleying along them will often be highly productive.

BELOW: Tidal outflows where dirty water meets bluewater are always worth fishing.

## TEMPERATURE CHANGES

Water temperature can be an important guide to catching game and sports fish. The only accurate way to measure water temperature is to have a gauge fitted to the dashboard or use a sounder with a temperature gauge fitted to the transducer or the hull.

Sea surface temperatures can change markedly and their effect on the fish in an area can be radical. There is no way of knowing this without a temperature gauge.

As an example, in our local area, we catch a lot of spotted and Spanish mackerel but are at the southern limit of their migration. If the water temperature falls below 21°C they won't bite but if it is say 25°C they bite their heads off.

A temperature gauge showing 20.5°C tells the anglers that mackerel are not worth chasing today. This same temperature tolerance applies to many fish.

Trolling around the open ocean often reveals marked variations in water temperature. Sometimes, all the strikes, particularly on yellowfin tuna, come from one particular temperature bracket.

If this is noticed, the skipper only needs to stay in that pocket of water to keep the strikes coming.

An accurate water temperature gauge is a valuable tool and can be used to catch more fish and avoids wasting time when target fish just won't bite or even be around at a prevailing temperature.

## REEF AND STRUCTURE

Any reef or underwater structure that disturbs or lifts the ocean current will attract bait fish and hold big fish.

Some of these places are world famous like the Grand Banks and Dogger Banks. Others are just

Ocean current swirling and boiling around offshore islands or shallow reefs provides a likely fishing spot.

islands in the sea which game and sportfish treat like an oasis in the desert.

Anywhere the ocean current runs into something or over something shallow, the fish will gather.

Both large pelagic fish and the reef dwellers like giant trevally, cobia, yellowtail kingfish, amberjack, mackerel, wahoo and so on will use these places, depending on the water depth and their location.

Working underwater geography takes a little knowledge and an application of proven technique to get the best results. The sounder shows its form and local knowledge will help to catch the fish that live there.

## WHITE WATER

Many sportfish are found around the coastal or coral edges marked by surf or breaking waves.

Trolling, lure casting or bait fishing around headlands, cliffs, islands, bommies and drop-offs is a popular and productive way to catch fish.

When working around white water always keep an eye on the sea as it can present real dangers in some locations.

## FLOATING OBJECTS

Anything substantial that floats around in the ocean will soon create an attendant web of life including the larger predators.

This includes timber or sometimes large trees and

Coral reefs with their deep drop-offs are always good fish producers.

## Bouys and beacons.

Direction of current

Mooring chain

Mooring block

## Fish trap floats for dolphin fish.

Direction of current

Larger fish often hold deeper and are more often taken on live baits

---

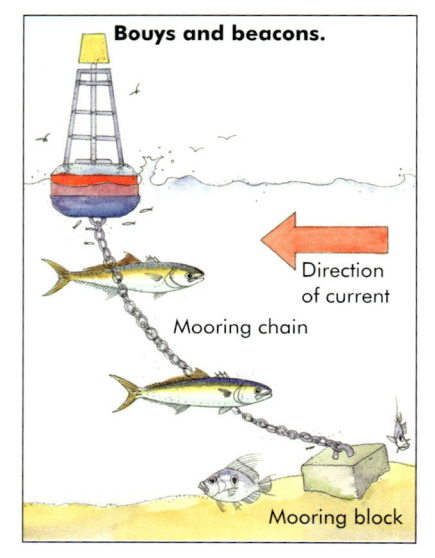

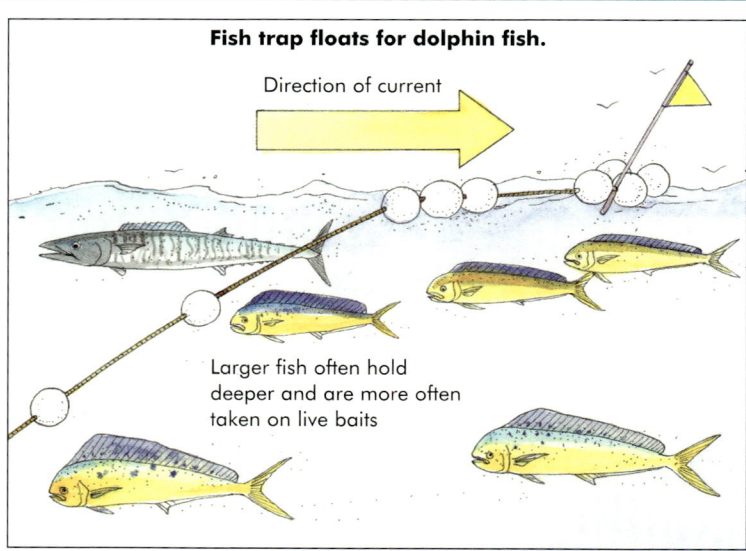

all sorts of things that float around the ocean. It also includes man made objects like fish trap floats, weather and wave rider buoys and navigation beacons.

All these things attract fish and are worth investigating.

Anglers and fisheries agencies around the world now lay their own floating objects anchored to the sea bed to attract game fish. These are known as Fish Aggregating Devices or FAD's.

The prime target of FAD's and other floating devices in tropical and temperate seas is dolphin fish (mahi mahi) which will gather around floating objects in big numbers.

Yellowfin and striped tuna (skipjack) will also gather and feed around such objects as will wahoo and marlin.

In NSW fish trap floats marking deepwater snapper and lobster traps often hold dolphin fish (mahi mahi), particularly if the floats have built up a growth of oceanic gooseneck barnacles.

Any substantial or permanent structures in the sea like large buoys also attract and hold big fish.

RIGHT: A NSW Fisheries FAD located in 100 metres of water off South West Rocks.

BELOW: The FAD in the background yielded this beautifully coloured dolphin fish.

BELOW: A FAD made from an old aircraft fuel tank and marked with a palm tree makes a striking sight off Sabah, east Borneo.

Inshore, navigation buoys and beacons leading into ports and harbours will hold yellowtail kingfish, amberjack, trevally and cobia as well as mackerel.

## SUNGLASSES

Polarising sunglasses are an essential tool on bluewater boats and they serve a range of purposes.

Their initial use was to allow deeper vision into the water. The polarising effect removing surface glare and allowing deeper, clearer vision.

This allowed anglers to see fish on sand flats and also bait fish, game fish and sharks far more clearly.

As the sky, sea and many of the fish appear as shades of blue the best shade of sunglasses to emphasise these colours is amber.

Protection from solar glare is also important. Quality polarising sunglasses offer good eye protection from the sun. This is important and helps avoid sore eyes, sunburnt eyes and glare induced headaches.

Finally, sunglasses can also help avoid physical damage to the eyes from rod tips, lures and flying hooks. Your author has had a lure come lose on a leaping marlin and has been hit hard right in the sunglasses by the hook set. Without the glasses serious damage could have been done.

Sunglasses are a tool of trade for offshore anglers and it is worth spending the money to buy good quality, well fitting glasses.

---

### FACT BOX

# FOLLOW THE SEASONS

Game fish are wanderers of the currents, they go where the ocean takes them and they also follow relatively well known migratory paths.

By learning these major fish movements anglers increase their chances of being in the right place at the right time.

Some places are famous for the concentration of fish present at particular times of the year. Cairns giant black marlin appear in September and run through to December. Broome's sailfish are thick from May to October. Bermagui's big yellowfin tuna are best in March, April and May. Eagle Hawk Neck in Tasmania has bluefin about the same time as Bermagui has yellowfin tuna.

This pattern is repeated right around the world and good anglers know when to apply techniques that work for the fish that are congregating or moving through their fishing area.

---

Bait fish rippling on the top will often have larger predators below.

Always fit the glasses with a pre-made safety string to keep them on your head when working over the side of the boat.

## BINOCULARS

A pair of waterproof binoculars can be extremely useful on any boat. They improve the visual range for the skipper and can help with catches.

On many occasions the binoculars can confirm things that the eye can just see, but can't properly work out what it is. Birds working, floating objects, fish or bait moving about at a distance and all sorts of bits and pieces.

They can also be used to steal information from other boats. If one boat is hooking fish after fish the binoculars can be used to check the rig or bait and then copy the successful boat.

Good anglers never stop learning and learning good ideas or rigs from others can always help.

## BIRDS

Seabirds can be a very good indicator of predatory fish working an area. The big fish push the bait fish

---

### FACT BOX

## DINNER BELLS

Oceanic game fish seem to feed at strangely irregular times.

Listening to radio scheds in game fishing tournaments sometimes provides interesting feedback.

Perhaps a hundred boats are out there fishing and each sched a handful of boats report a strike or a fish. All this goes on a log sheet.

Then for some reason at a particular sched lots of boats will be hooked up and hook ups may continue for an hour or two then fade back to a few an hour.

Why this happens out on a big seemingly featureless ocean is anyone's guess but game fish do have 'feeding times'. We tend to correlate them mostly with tide change times but there is room for considerable speculation.

---

Sea birds feeding at the surface are always a sign of action happening below.

# FINDING FISH

Sea birds wheeling and diving are a certain indicator of fish feeding below.

involved with feeding fish at times.

Flocks of birds can be located on radar and tuna anglers use their radar to find the groups of wheeling birds and then the tuna that are feeding under them.

Those without radar need good eyes scanning the horizon looking for the telltale signs.

Learning a bit about seabirds can pay dividends for alert anglers and they are an important sign post in the sea.

to the surface as they attack them and the birds then join in the feast.

When fish are feeding the birds tend to pack in tightly as they dive and wheel to feed on the bait.

Sometimes the birds are just doing what the anglers are doing, searching and looking for a feed.

Picking the difference can be important to catches.

The best seabirds indicators for anglers are terns of various types, shearwaters, petrels and gannets. All these birds are very bait fish orientated.

Seagulls are basically rats with wings and rarely indicate fish, albatross don't get too involved with schools of fish and many of the smaller birds like prions and others are plankton feeders, though they do get

## BAIT BALLS

Bait balls are sometimes found on the surface but more often are located on the sounder. These bait balls are very regularly under attack by game fish.

A range of fishing techniques has been developed to catch the game fish that gather around these bait shows (See chapter 6).

The important point is to recognise the telltale signs either on the surface or on the sounder and then present baits or lures to hook the fish. Once the bait fish are located and appropriate techniques applied, the strike often follows quickly, because the game fish are right on the bait. Adding seemingly injured ones to a school of healthy bait gets the big fish going.

Small tuna attacking pilchards are easy to see.

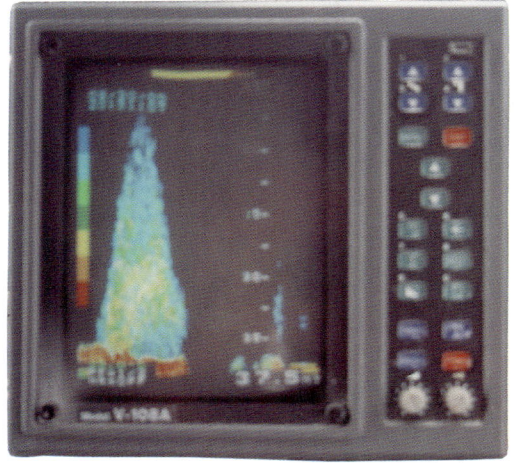

Modern colour sounders often locate bait balls which can then be worked for game fish.

Big lures, big reels and big bent butt game rods mean big marlin.
PHOTO: GLEN BOOTH

# CHAPTER 4

# LURE TROLLING FOR BIG GAME FISH

Lure trolling at sea actually has a handful of sub-sections, with a little knowledge of all of them needed to get the best out of any situation.

Trolling lures is an ancient art, wherever people travelled in boats they learnt to troll lures. Today it has developed into something of a science. These developments have occurred mostly in the big fish type trolling lures where there has been great interest in tuna and billfish trolling right around the world.

## BIG FISH TROLLING

Starting at the top end, big fish trolling has a large number of enthusiastic supporters. It is popular because it is a simple operation that can and does attract big fish and often yields marlin, sailfish, spearfish, tuna, dolphin fish (mahi mahi) and wahoo.

## SKIRTED LURES

Lures for game fish have been hugely developed over the past decade to a point where there are lures of every possible shape, size and colour available.

Their actions in the water are governed in the main by the shape of the lure's head or face and the trolling speed.

How each of these lures work when trolled relates to how water runs over the head of the lure. This provides both lure action and a bubble trail as the lure breaks through the surface and drags air back under the water with it.

A close look at the various types of lure heads gives some understanding to how they work.

ABOVE: Trolling an assortment of lures and different types of tackle can provide a wide range of game fish.

Outriggers and rod holders maximise the opportunities for bluewater trolling.

RIGHT: Offshore lure trolling.

*A black marlin with its attendant remora caught on a cup faced lure.*

Pointy lures built much like squid run straight and have very little action. They may have plastic or metal heads sometimes with holes to enhance the bubble trail. They don't like high speeds as they have little grip on the water and work best at 6 to 8 knots. Because of this lack of grip they tend to be easily blown sideways in cross-winds, which can cause tangles.

Despite their lack of action in the water, these lures are particularly effective on tuna and wahoo and are good takers of billfish.

Angled or sliced heads are a development of the original Kona Head designs. The angled face of the lure provides it with action and surface breaks as it is towed along. A wide number of variations on this theme exists although the principle that makes them work remains the same.

*A solid yellowfin tuna taken on a traditional konahead lure.*

These lures tend to work best at medium speeds of 6 to 9 knots and they are reliable fish catchers.

Cup faced lures bite into the water surface and use a combination of air and water for their sometimes considerable action. Cup face lures also tend to travel a little deeper when they plunge under the surface which may lead to some extra attractiveness to the fish. These lures work at 7 to 12 knots and are one of the most popular styles on billfish.

Flat face type lures work similarly to cup faced lures and are particularly common in the moulded soft head type lures. These lures have a high success rate and the soft bodied lures are often struck repeatedly by attacking fish as their lifelike 'feel' does not alert the fish that the lure is a fake.

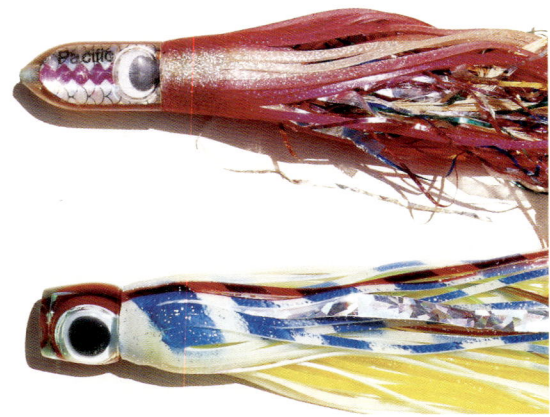

*Comparison with a cup face and a round design. Cup face lures bite the water and hold position. Rounded head lures have no grip on the water and are easliy blown sideways by cross winds.*

High speed trolling lures have a small, flat or cupped shaped face on a thin tapered head and a plastic skirt tail. They work well at conventional speeds however their thin profile allows them to be towed at speeds up to 15 knots and they are a handy lure when travelling.

Metal headed lures like jet heads and hex heads are also popular in many places. These lures are basically similar to moulded plastic type heads but are made from turned or milled metal.

The extra weight of metal headed lures (particularly in the larger sizes) often lets them run fractionally deeper in the water and they often 'grip' the water very well.

For reasons known only to the fish, hex head type lures have an extremely high strike rate on wahoo. They are also a good lure for windy days as they hold their place in a pattern very well.

## COLOURED SKIRTS

While the head shape of a lure determines its action and movement in the water it is the skirt that gives it colour and its bait fish illusion in the water.

Most skirts are vinyl or plastic with a silicon base to keep them supple. They come in a vast array of colours and shades and anglers need to chose the colours they like or know to be popular fish catching colours.

Trying to dictate colour to any lure trolling angler is a waste of breath or ink. Everyone develops lure makes, sizes and colours that work for them.

It is human nature I guess, but there are trends that flow through the fishing information system which should not be ignored.

For new anglers learning the craft, look at what the successful anglers or charter boats are using and start there. Talk about lure selection and skirt colours with anglers who know what they are doing or at local tackle shops.

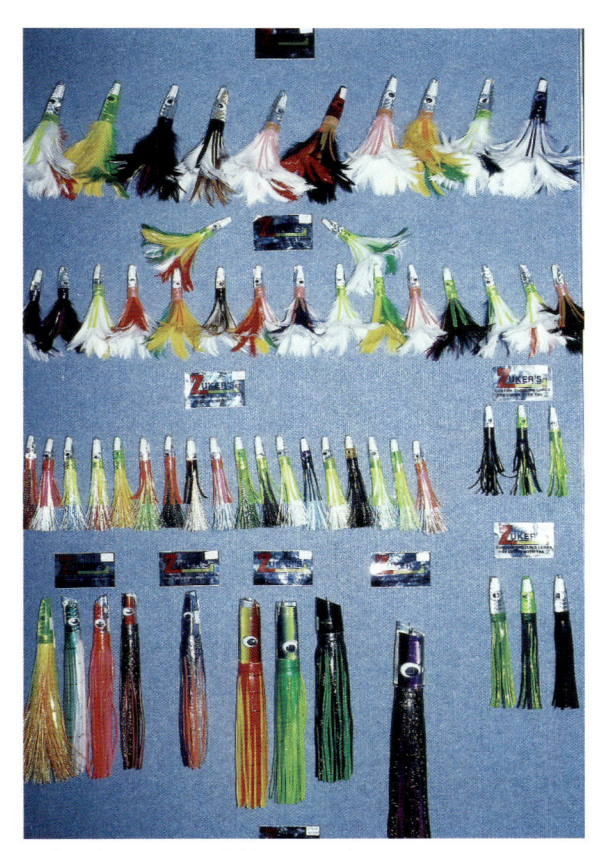

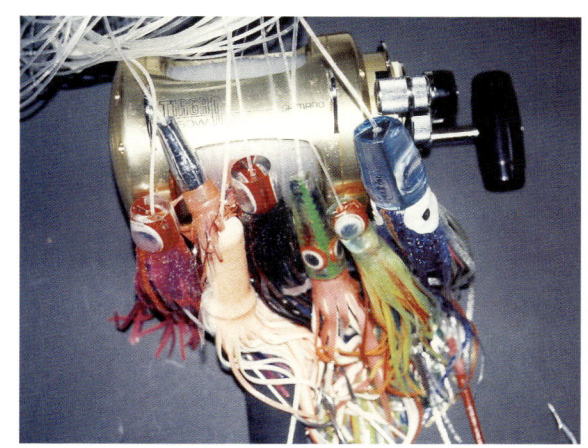

You don't need lots of lures just a selection of the ones that work will be enough.

Trolling lures are available in just about every size, shape, colour and pattern imaginable. Anglers need to learn what colours, shapes and sizes work best in their fishing area.

Matching the most common bait fish in any area for size and colour is always a good start. If it is slimy mackerel then green, blue and silver is good. If it is flying fish then shades of blue may be good. Frigate mackerel or small striped tuna (skipjack) are matched with black. Squid are matched with pink, reds and browns.

If lots of small bait are around use small lures. If the bait fish appear large then work larger lures.

Once on the water, if one lure colour or size keeps getting hit, the answer is to put out another one just the same. If it keeps happening repeat the dose.

It's all about trolling something that the game fish, no matter how big or small, relate to as food items and they eat it.

Lure skirts are easily changed if they are damaged and learning to do this is part of the craft. Most tackle shops and lure manufacturers will also change the skirts for you. The key is to get the right sized skirts and then glue them into position.

The skirts can also be kept soft and supple with a wash in fresh water and a spray with silicon conditioner every couple of months.

## RIGGING BIG FISH LURES

Heavy duty nylon crimping systems have made rigging big fish lures a relatively simple task.

Most lures are rigged on about 4 metres of trace, with the trace length used depending on personal preference and the size of the fish being chased. Bigger fish may require longer traces, up to 6 metres, but it depends on how each crew works their tracing and gaffing. If using wind-on traces, the lures are rigged on short 1 metre (3 foot) traces.

## TRACE

The trace size used to rig trolling lures relates to both the size of the lure, the size fish expected and the tackle being used.

Big lures need heavy trace, because big fish can be expected. Heavy gear needs heavy trace to cope with the stress and wear factors imposed. The heavier the tackle used the greater the wear that impacts on the trace.

As a rule of thumb, small to medium size lures for marlin and tuna up to 100 kg (200 lb) can be rigged on 150 lb to 250 lb trace. Lures for larger marlin are generally rigged on 300 to 400 lb trace. Anglers chasing marlin in excess of 250 kg (500 lb) often use traces around 600lb to handle these large fish beside the boat.

While there are anglers who state that some marlin are put off by heavy traces and light traces will increase the strike ratio your authors have seen little or no sign of this. We have however seen a couple of big fish lost through the trace being too light and wearing out in a protracted fight.

## HOOKS

The hooks used are always straight patterns, (with no kirb or set) like Mustad 7731, 7732S, 7691S or 7766. Many anglers use stainless steel hooks for their rust free convenience, others use chemically sharpened hooks for their razor sharpness, while others use standard steel patterns for their ability to hold a sharp point and their comparatively low cost.

Both stainless and mild steel patterns always need work with a file to make them ultra sharp. From a personal point of view we mostly use Mustad stainless 76LGS or 7691S hooks and have good results.

Be careful using chemically sharpened hooks when trolling they can and do lose their points due to electrolysis over time.

## ONE HOOK OR TWO

This argument has many angles to it and it depends on the fish and fishing style being used and personal choice. If yellowfin or bluefin tuna are the target then a single hook at the back end of the skirt is by far the best option. On tuna keep the hooks small with 6/0 to 8/0 in the small to medium lure sizes and 9/0 and 10/0 in the larger sizes.

On marlin most anglers favour a two hook rig particularly on the larger lures from 25 cm (10 ins) long and upwards. One medium sized hook seems to work best on the smaller lures rather than two small hooks.

The hooks can also be set at different angles to improve the hook-up rate although most anglers tend to use both points facing up towards the surface. The hooks can also be set so one point faces up and one point faces down.

The heavy hooks used in this form of trolling can kill the lure action particularly on small lures. Big hooks are also very hard to drive home on light tackle so take care choosing hook sizes. Trolling type hooks are very strong but always relate the hook size and strength to the tackle being used.

Smaller to medium lures work best with 6/0 to 8/0 size hooks irrespective of the line class used. On gear of 15 to 24 kg (30 to 50 lb), better results will be achieved using 9/0's and 10/0's rather than bigger sizes even on quite large lures. When big lures on heavy tackle are being towed the hooks need to be 12/0 to 14/0 to cope with the size and physical strength of the fish.

## RIGGING THE LURE

The trace is made up using a stainless thimble at the lure end with a rubber washer set on the trace above the crimp. The washer beds the lure down and holds it in place while trolling.

On smaller lures a hook is added by way of a small shackle. On longer lures a short trace is made up on 600 lb multistrand stainless wire to connect the hook to the shackle.

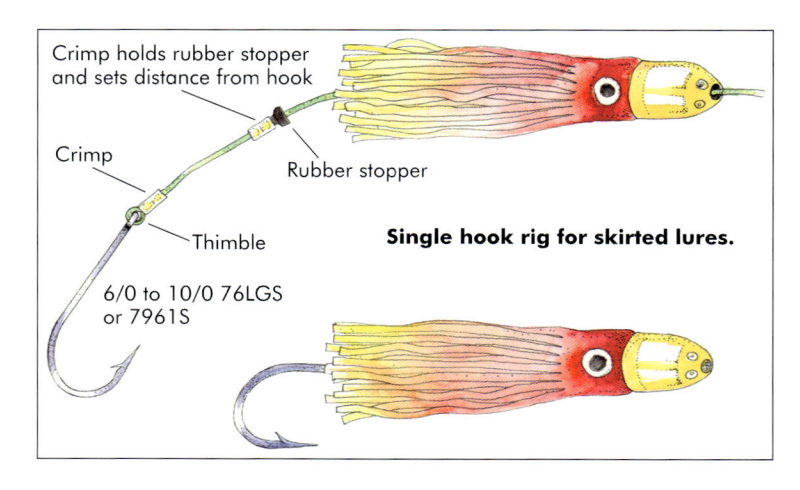

**Single hook rig for skirted lures.**

Crimp holds rubber stopper and sets distance from hook

Crimp

Rubber stopper

Thimble

6/0 to 10/0 76LGS or 7961S

**Rigging the lure.**

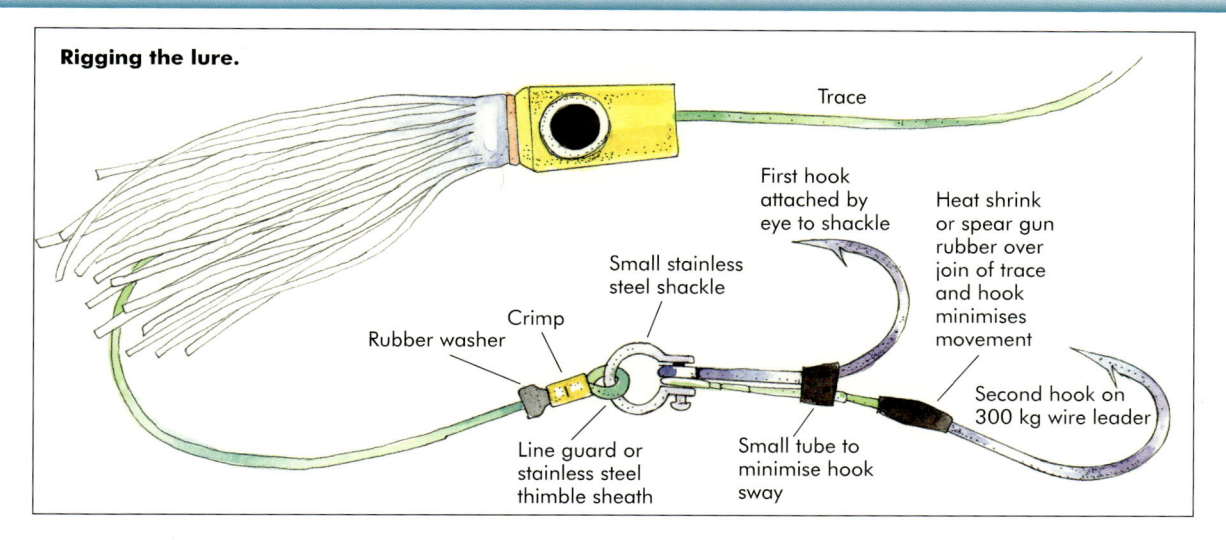

*Labels: Trace; First hook attached by eye to shackle; Heat shrink or spear gun rubber over join of trace and hook minimises movement; Small stainless steel shackle; Second hook on 300 kg wire leader; Crimp; Rubber washer; Line guard or stainless steel thimble sheath; Small tube to minimise hook sway*

Light gauge heat shrink tubing or spear gun rubber is used to stiffen the link between the hook and the trace. This actually stops the hook from swinging around on the trace, which can work harden the wire leading to eventual breakage.

When a second hook is required it is secured by placing the shackle pin through the eye of the hook. A small piece of plastic tubing, heat shrink or rubber then links the first hook to the trace of the back hook minimising sway.

By rigging this way, a lure can carry one or two hooks just by using the small shackle. Hook sizes can also be easily changed to suit the line class being fished.

This rigging method also allows lures to be rigged and carried without hooks and means only 20 or so hooks are needed to maintain a wide selection of lures.

## SETTING THE PATTERN

Big fish trolling relies on a pattern of lures to maximise strikes. The boat is probably the first thing the fish sees although many big fish seem to be drawn like a magnet to a particular lure and are rarely scared of the boat.

On marlin, four or five lures in the pattern is enough as things can be very difficult if a jumping fish takes the lure close to the boat and then weaves its way out through the other outfits.

When marlin trolling, a teaser, bird or similar device that adds action in amongst the lures can help draw extra strikes. From our experience it is hard to beat a Pakula Witchdoctor or similar teaser beating and flashing just in front of the first big fish lure.

How the lures are arranged is a matter of preference and a bit of experience.

Some anglers like to work the lures in matched pairs down each side of the boat while others like to have a long side and short side. With a short corner rod matched with a short lure in the outrigger and a long corner rod matched by a long line on the rigger.

The fifth lure is usually set down the middle of the

**Outrigger tag lines for skirted lures.**

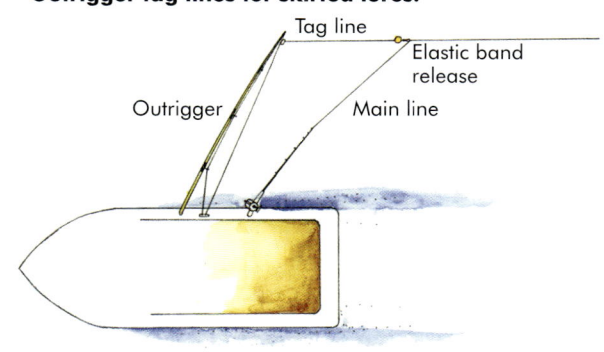

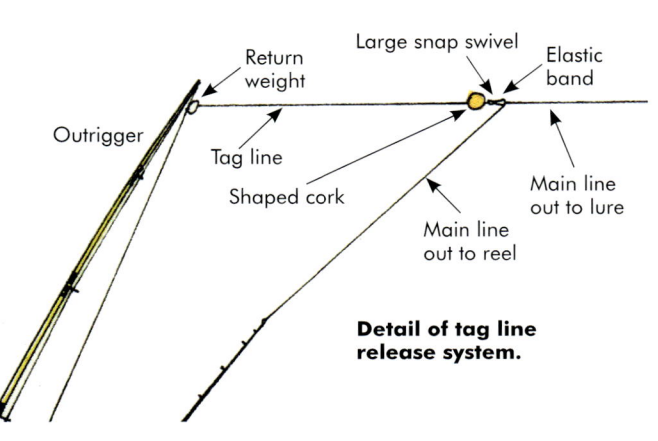

*Labels: Tag line; Elastic band release; Outrigger; Main line*

*Labels: Return weight; Large snap swivel; Elastic band; Outrigger; Tag line; Shaped cork; Main line out to lure; Main line out to reel*

**Detail of tag line release system.**

**Lure trolling pattern for marlin.**

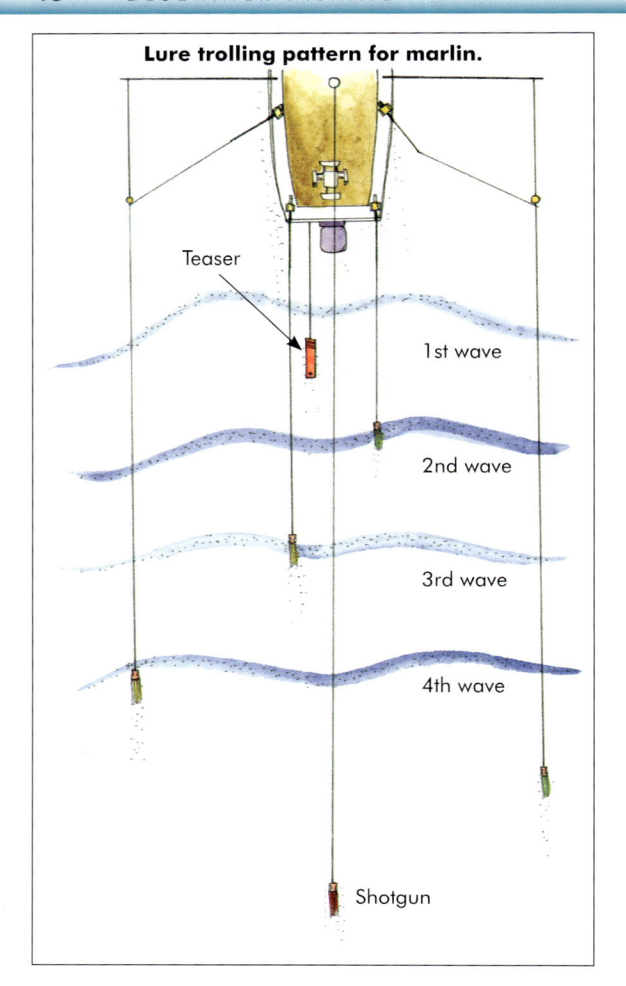

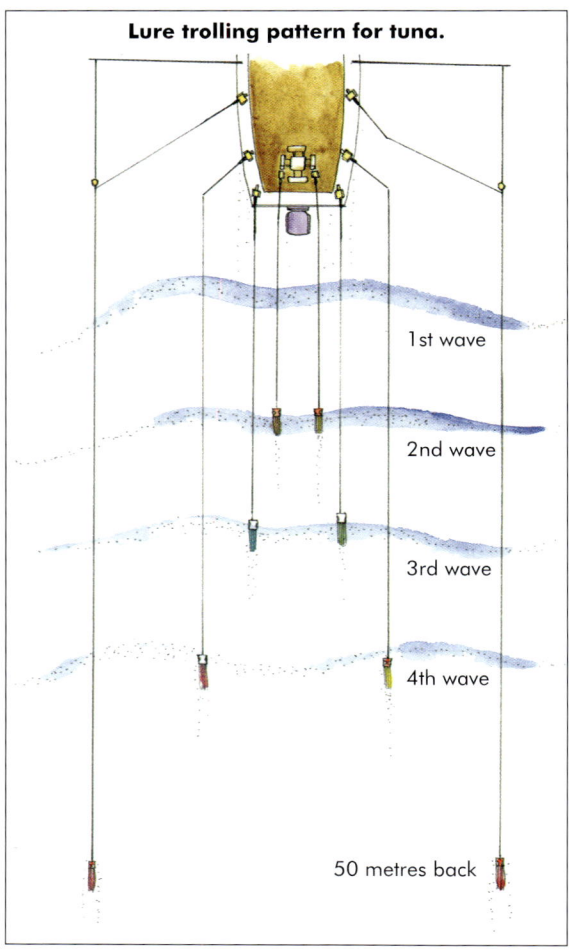

Teaser
1st wave
2nd wave
3rd wave
4th wave
Shotgun

**Lure trolling pattern for tuna.**

1st wave
2nd wave
3rd wave
4th wave
50 metres back

pattern and behind the other lures with the rod in the rocket launcher, this is known as the 'shotgun' lure.

Our best results on marlin have come from using a five lure pattern with two short lures run from the stern corners, (about 25 metres or 75 feet) two outrigger lures set at around 50 metres (150 feet) and the fifth lure run down the centre of the wake but kept slightly shorter than the outrigger lures.

The short lures and the outrigger lures are set as matched pairs.

The pattern looks a little like a five face on a dice, with the centre dot dropped back a little.

The advantage of this pattern is that it is almost tangle free and allows for manoeuvring around fish attractors, schools of bait, islands or whatever without fuss.

All lures are set on top of the wake rolls behind the boat. The wake roll optically enhances the appearance and the movement of the lure to any fish swimming below. The effect is like putting something in the centre of a glass lens. Lures can be set in the second, third and so on wake rolls.

Even though it looks close many fish are caught in the second or third wake roll close to the boat, so don't think all the lures need to be way back, they don't.

Lure patterns are set very deliberately and attention should be paid to lure placement. Some lures simply work and catch better in particular spots in the pattern. Most of this is only discovered by experience and strike rates.

When deliberately chasing yellowfin and bluefin tuna, it is possible, if boat space permits, to troll eight or more rods. This is because tuna are a school fish and the more lures out the back the better the chances of multiple hook-ups when a school is contacted.

Tuna usually run deep on the strike and any crossovers of other lines can be quickly sorted out.

On tuna it is usual to put two or three lures on wakes two and three and then two lures out the back

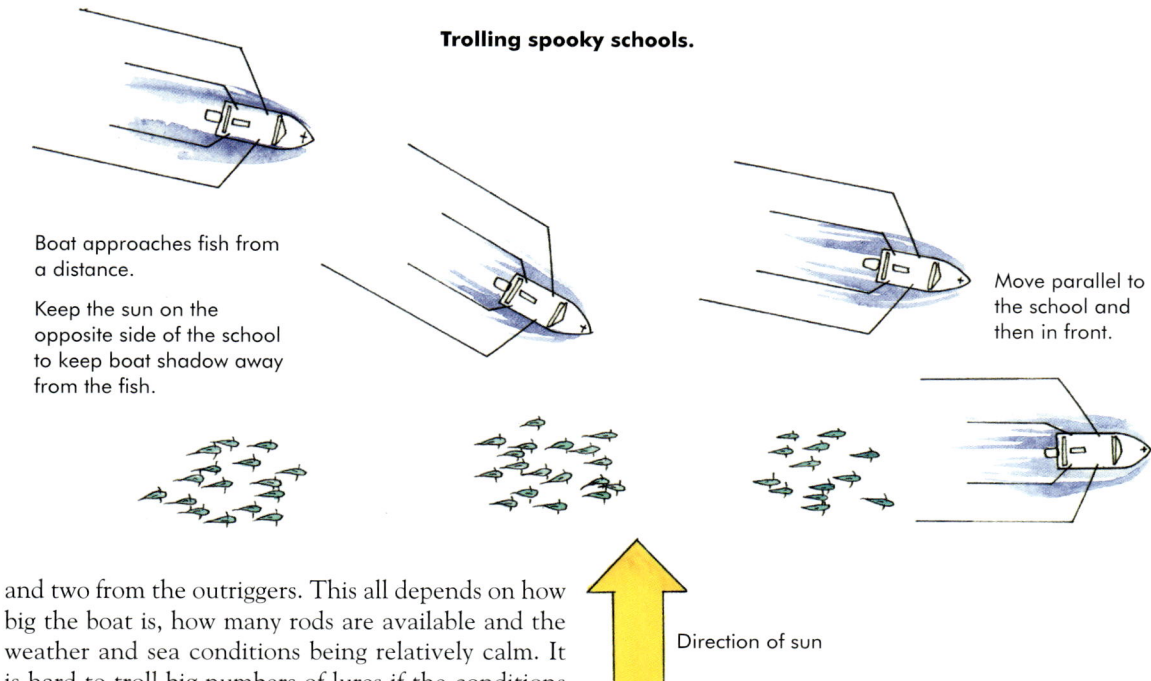

# LURE TROLLING FOR BIG GAME FISH

**Trolling spooky schools.**

Boat approaches fish from a distance.

Keep the sun on the opposite side of the school to keep boat shadow away from the fish.

Move parallel to the school and then in front.

Direction of sun

and two from the outriggers. This all depends on how big the boat is, how many rods are available and the weather and sea conditions being relatively calm. It is hard to troll big numbers of lures if the conditions are difficult.

When the tuna strike, keep the boat going forward for at least 100 metres as the rest of the school will often start hooking up.

## DRAG SETTINGS

Drag settings when trolling lures is an often debated topic and there are a couple of options.

The most commonly used method is to troll the lure with the outfits set at strike drag. This way the fish hits the lure and the hooks are driven home by the forward motion of the boat.

Once the fish is running, the angler takes the rod and fights the fish.

Some anglers use a light, say 2 kg (4 lb) drag setting and then set the hooks after the fish takes the lure and runs off.

Both methods work but we prefer everything to come tight immediately and stay that way. There is room here for variations and anglers can experiment to find a sytem that works best for them.

Our drag settings when lure trolling are always more than a quarter but less than one third of the breaking strain of the line.

This ensures a firm hook up but lets the fish run without breaking the line. Applying more than one third of the line breaking strain as drag will usually break the line. (See Setting the Drag page 113).

As a side issue, it is almost impossible to hook big fish on lures with a hand held rod. Always have the outfit in the rod holder when trolling, it provides the best hook ups.

## BLUEWATER MINNOWS

While conventional skirted lures are excellent fish catchers they are not the only answer. Large minnows with their sub surface swimming action are also highly attractive to game fish.

The main targets with minnows in open bluewater are yellowfin and bluefin tuna and wahoo. Billfish regularly attack these lures but the relatively small double and treble hooks do not hook or hold billfish well.

However when tuna or wahoo are the target the minnows provide excellent results.

In near coastal trolling, around washes, headlands, bommies, coral drop offs and islands, minnow type lures are extremely effective.

Fish like tailor, salmon, bonito, yellowtail kingfish, cobia, trevally, queenfish, mackerel and barracuda are highly attracted to the swimming, fish profiles of minnow lures.

There are two basic types of minnows, those with

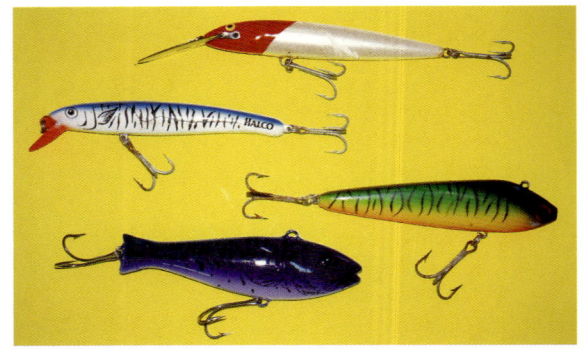

ABOVE: Wahoo are highly attracted to trolled minnow lures.

ABOVE LEFT: A school yellowfin caught on a minnow lure is played to the boat.

LEFT: Bibbed and bibless minnows used for offshore trolling.

bibs which impart the swimming action and those with a body shape and balance point which gives the lure a shimmy, vibrating action. These are known as bibless minnows.

Both types of minnows work and it can be a matter of application to test for best results. Bibless type lures can generally be trolled faster and run straighter than the longer bodied minnows.

The lures also come in a wide range of shapes and sizes and have widely differing hooks sizes and strengths. Always match the lures to the tackle being used and fit the lures with extra strong treble hooks.

Mixing minnow lures in a pattern of skirted lures can cause a few problems because both lure types move differently through the water.

Always allow room for the extra movement in the water of minnows when setting a lure pattern.

In some conditions and situations it is often better to just troll only minnows or only skirted lures.

## RIGGING BLUEWATER MINNOWS

As billfish rarely stay connected on minnows the trace for tuna is usually 2 metres (6 ft) of 40 kg (80 lb) nylon with a snap swivel on one end and a solid brass ring on the other. This allows for rapid lure changes and easy attachment to standard game and sportfishing tackle. Move the trace size up to 75 kg (150 lb) if the tuna are large.

For wahoo and mackerel, 30 to 50 kg (60 to 100 lb) wire trace rigged basically the same way as for tuna will prevent bite offs. The wire can be as short as 30 cm (12 ins) if desired and then backed up by 40 kg (80 lb) nylon. The main issue is keeping the fishes' teeth off tender nylon when it attacks the lure.

# OTHER TACTICS

## TEASERS FOR TROLLING

Teasers are used as attractors to draw fish to the boat and to excite the fish into striking either the baits or lures being trolled.

They work by providing splash or flash or both and are generally fished on cord lines without hooks.

There are three main types of teasers; birds, daisy chains and witchdoctors.

## BIRDS

Birds are plastic or wooden fish shaped lures with rigid extended wings on each side. When pulled through the water these wings flutter madly giving off signals

## FACT BOX

## LURE COLOUR COUNTS

Lure colours can make a big difference to catches as some colours just seem to work better than others.

Some of the colour selections seem to work everywhere and are thus universally attractive to fish.

Other colours are more area specific and relate to bait fish found in various regions.

In areas with high flying fish numbers dark blue lures will get a lot of attention.

More generally, there has been a lure fishing maxim of dark lures on light days and light coloured lures on dark days.

Our experience tends to favour the use of generally attractive coloured lures on all days regardless of the light conditions.

Lure and colour selection can be personal but our favourites would fit into the following ten colour schemes. Lure size, head shape and action also count as much as colour.

### TOP TEN

1. Blue, silver, green (Evil pattern)
2. Black over dark blue (or its reverse)
3. Hot pink over white and/or with tinsel
4. Red over white
5. Lumo green (yellowfin tuna special)
6. Dark blue over white
7. Yellow over green (dolphin fish (mahi mahi) special)
8. Copper/gold over purple ( bluefin tuna)
9. Pink over purple or pink over mauve
10. Black over lime green (wahoo special)

Any pattern with combinations of the above will hook fish, the rest is up to the angler.

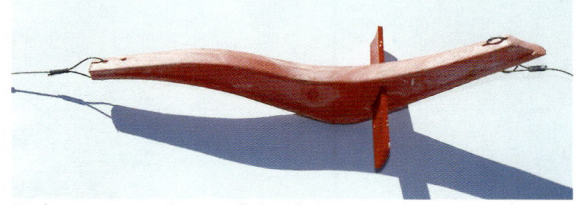

*Bird type teasers have a flying fish type action across the surface of the water.*

bird like a kite tail and can be particularly useful if the sea is a little choppy.

Birds work best in smooth to moderate seas but have problems in rough water as they leave the water surface and tangle easily in these conditions.

Birds work best at slower trolling speeds of 4 to 8 knots and are at their most effective when combined with bait trolling.

## DAISY CHAINS

These are basically strings of lures set on one length of heavy line. Usually plastic squids or softhead type pushers are used.

*Daisy chains add a bait fish school appearance to the wake of the vessel.*

similar to a distressed fish or flying fish desperately trying to lift off the surface.

The birds can be trolled by themselves or with a lure or string of lures (usually plastic squids) trailing behind them. These added lures help stabilise the

# 50 BLUEWATER FISHING

Daisy chains are mostly used when chasing sailfish and small marlin and provide an image of numerous small fish following the boat.

Generally, two daisy chains (one each side) of five lures each are used with the baits or lures set both beside and behind the attractors.

Daisy chains will work when combined with lures or baits at speeds of 5 to 10 knots and they are effective attractors. They can also be a good way of using accumulated lures which are not in general use.

The chains are simple to make with a big swivel at the top for connection to some venetian blind cord and the lures threaded onto some 400 lb nylon trace and held in place with a crimp. The end is secured with a metal thimble or ring.

Spreader bars are an enhanced form of daisy chain. These stainless bars or wires allow for up to 5 daisy chains to be towed off each spreader. Some boats tow numerous spreader bars to provide a wake that appears full of bait fish.

## WITCHDOCTOR

The Witchdoctor was invented by lure maker Peter Pakula and is basically a piece of 2" X 4" timber with an angled face and a towing eye. The timber is brightly painted and large mirror surfaces are attached to each flat side.

The teaser is set on strong cord, and towed about 20 metres (60 ft) behind the boat.

When towed by the boat the Witchdoctor dives to about 2 metres (6 ft) and then works with a powerful side to side beat, its mirrored surface sending out flashes of light through the water layers.

Witchdoctors have a great success rate on marlin and the lure set nearest the Witchdoctor regularly receives the most strikes which is an indicator of its power of attraction.

Teasers add extra fish to the catch by both attracting them from either further away or further down in the water column and by exciting them to strike.

They are worth using when chasing big fish, particularly marlin and sailfish.

Pakula witchdoctor.

# TROLLING BAITS

A mixture of swimming and skipping baits works best and gives the fish a choice of baits to hit and plenty of visual targets.

Rigged baits and live baits also work well from downriggers and one downrigger should be a consideration. It does not need to be fancy, just a 5 kg (10 lb) downrigger weight set on 200 kg (400 lb) venetian blind cord can be used for starters and this will happily work a bait at 10 metres (30 ft) down.

The weight is hauled in when the strike becomes a hook up.

The key to successful bait trolling is to work at it. Get the rigs right for the bait fish available in your fishing area and then apply it to the fish and the results will come.

**Suggested pattern for trolling with bait.**

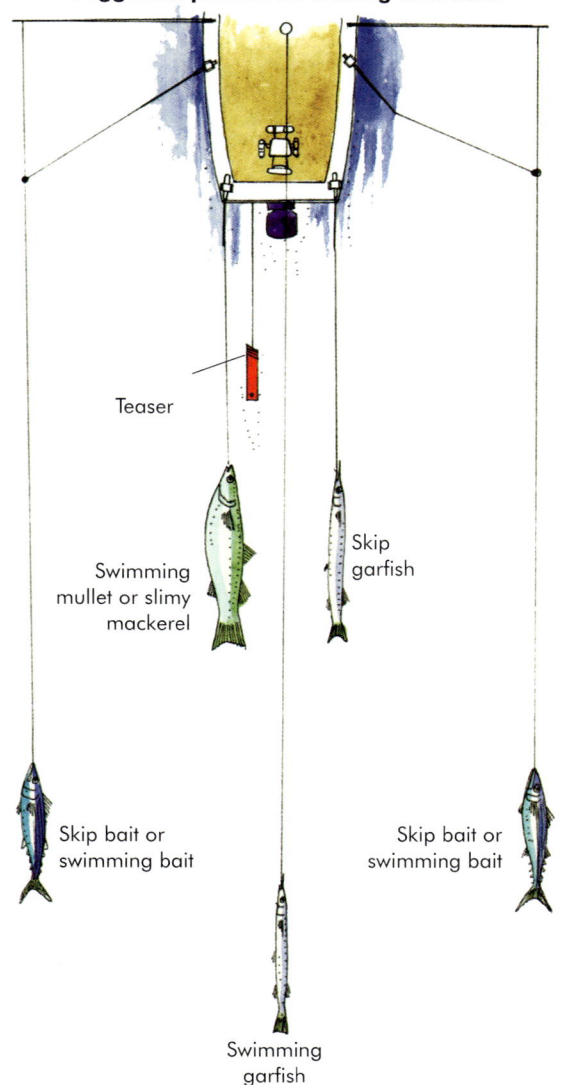

Teaser

Swimming mullet or slimy mackerel

Skip garfish

Skip bait or swimming bait

Skip bait or swimming bait

Swimming garfish

## RIG 1

# DAVE'S SKIP BAIT

This is the easiest and one of the most deadly rigs ever invented. Despite all the flash skip bait rigs, this one delivers the hook cleanly into fish and is almost too simple for many people to use.

Make up the trace using 8/0 or 10/0 Mustad 9175 hooks and sharpen them. The trace is usually about 3 or 4 metres (9–12 ft) long and is finished with a solid brass ring. For most applications 100 kg to 150 kg (200–300 lb) nylon trace will work fine. If hammerhead sharks are about and the anglers want to catch and tag them add 30 cm (12 ins) of nylon coated 75 kg (150 lb) wire and join with oversize crimps. (See Combination Traces).

Hammerhead sharks are absolute suckers for skip baits.

### STEPS

**1** Use a bait needle to sew the mouth and gills shut. This stops water entry which may eventually destroy the bait.

**2** Use a frigate mackerel, small tuna, bonito, cowanyoung, scad or large slimy mackerel and place the hook under the bottom jaw and bring the point out through the nose near the front but just behind the mouth parts.

**3** Pull the hook into place and flex the bait. The bait is now ready to troll and will skip along happily at 4 to 6 knots depending on sea conditions.

These baits work best from an outrigger with plenty of drop back but can be worked on flatlines. Fish the reels with just enough drag to prevent an overrun on the strike and allow the fish time to swallow the bait before striking.

This rig is highly suited for circle hooks and 13/0 to 15/0 circles will yield good hook-ups on billfish.

# RIG 2

# INSHORE GANG RIGS

Inshore sportfish like tailor, salmon, yellowtail kingfish, cobia and mackerel are regular takers of trolled baits. In many cases trolled baits can be far more productive than lures, though this depends on how the fish are feeding.

One of the simplest yet most effective rigs is a moulded piece of lead set on ganged hooks. These pre-made rigs allow the rapid rigging and trolling of garfish, pike, pilchards, wolf herring and belly strips.

## BAIT BALLS

Bait balls are the best fish attractor in the ocean. Sometimes they are small concentrations of bait but they can also be significant and long lasting aggregations of small fish.

**Live bait trolling pattern.**

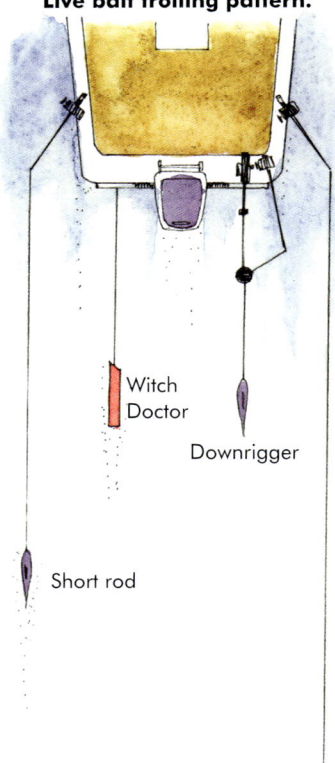

Witch Doctor
Downrigger
Short rod
Long rod

Some of these rigs tend to be area specific and are developed to suit the taste of the local fish population or local fishing techniques.

### STEPS

**1** Pin the bait to the gang with the last hook going through the head or eye sockets of the bait fish.

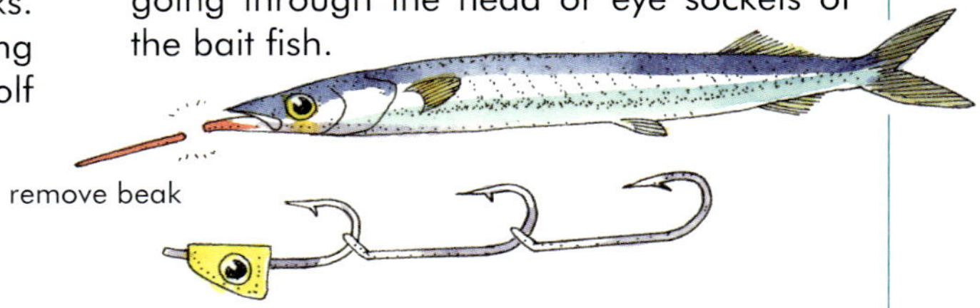

remove beak

**2** Lock the mouth or head to the rig with soft copper wire where needed.

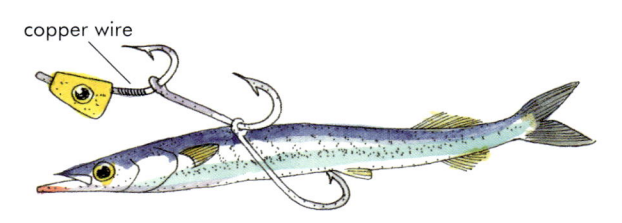

copper wire

**3** A nylon or wire trace is used depending on the target species.

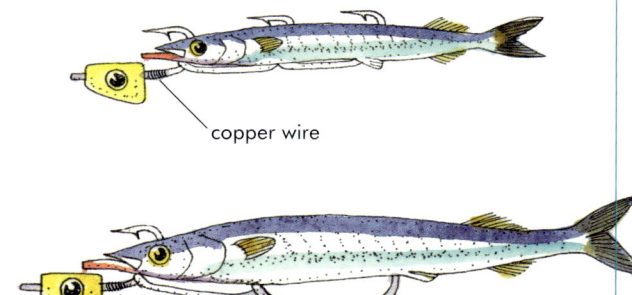

copper wire

copper wire

These rigs are usually towed at 3 to 5 knots with the reel set at strike drag so the attacking fish has the hooks driven home as they hit the bait.

## RIG 3

# SWIMMING GARFISH

This rig can be run on nylon or .022 single strand wire depending on the toothy critter population of the area. In temperate waters worked on nylon traces it is dynamite on yellowtail kingfish, yellowfin tuna, dolphin fish (mahi mahi), tuna and marlin. In tropical waters the same bait worked on wire will catch everything from coral trout, trevally and mackerel through to marlin and sailfish.

The key to the rig is a 1.5 cm (½ ins) sprig of .022 or .024 single strand wire which holds the garfish in place. A small elastic band locks the garfish onto the rig. The rigs are made up before going fishing and the garfish are buttoned on and used in a matter of seconds.

The monofilament rig is made using the sleeve above the hook to hold the sprig of wire. The wire is set on top of the mono so that it will be absolutely in line with the curve of the hook when it is bent at right angles once the crimp is closed. Trace sizes should be 50 kg (100 lb) for yellowtail kingfish and tuna and 100 kg to 150 kg (200 to 300 lb) for marlin.

Needle Eye Tarpon pattern hooks in 6/0 to 8/0 are used. A No. 2 or No. 3 size Bean sinker is added, this acts as a keel, and a plastic squid is optional, depending on personal preference. The rig is finished with a solid brass ring at the connecting end of the trace. If a skipping gar is required, use the same rig without lead.

When the rig is made on single strand wire the sprig is trimmed to size and left in place on completion of the haywire twist and barrel roll. The gar is then set on the rig as illustrated.

Needle Eye hooks are used where possible as they sit better in rigged baits than traditional hooks with round eyes. They tend not to break up the bait as round eye hooks can do.

If a plastic squid has been added, slide this down over the head of the garfish. This bait can be fished on either a firm drag for instant hook up or a light drag to allow the fish to swallow the bait. The authors prefer a firm drag and let all fish, including marlin, run into a firm drag. Only sailfish need a bit of time to swallow the bait.

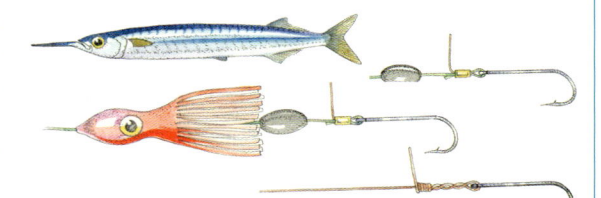

Various rigs to be used with the garfish rig.

### Steps

1 Flex and stretch the garfish to make it supple, and then snip the bill off.

2 Open the gill cover and bend the head of the gar over. This allows the hook point to travel as far as possible into the gut section of the garfish.

3 Push the hook out through the centre line on the belly of the garfish.

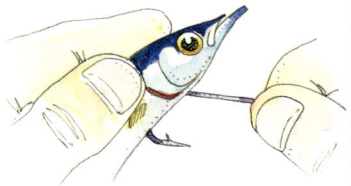

4 Once the hook is pulled inside the garfish, push the wire through the bottom jaw and out through the top of the mouth absolutely dead centre on the bait.

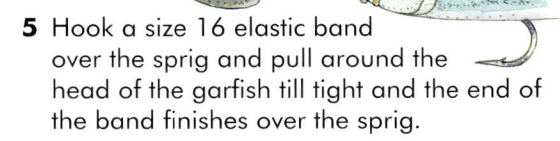

5 Hook a size 16 elastic band over the sprig and pull around the head of the garfish till tight and the end of the band finishes over the sprig.

6 Slide the sinker under the garfish's chin and it will swim deliciously straight at 4 to 7 knots.

## RIG 4

# SWIMMING BAITS

As the name implies swimming baits move through the water just like a fish. Their movements are often exaggerated but the game fish find them highly attractive.

To achieve a swimming action the bait is made supple by removing all or part of the spine either through the gut cavity or by using a sharpened metal tube to 'core' the bait.

Swimming baits are not difficult to rig but they are fiddly. Rigging them on a bait table on a large game boat is relatively simple but the same job in the confines of a pitching small boat is much more difficult.

In many cases it is best to pre-rig the baits on land and freeze them in packs of 5 or 6, and take them to sea ready to use.

Mullet, scad, bonito, frigate mackerel, pike and slimy mackerel can all be rigged to 'swim' as can almost any other bait fish. The only way to become proficient at bait rigging is to do it regularly.

Swimming baits can be worked from either outriggers or flatlines and a drop back or controlled minimum drag is used to allow the fish time to take and swallow the bait.

There are myriad variations on this rig and it can be rigged on wire for inshore predators like mackerel. Hook placement can also take place via the anal vent by using a pre-made extension trace to link the hook with the trace passing through the head. Again this variation is mostly used for mackerel fishing.

### Steps

1 Remove the gills and gut by opening the gill but do not break the neck membrane.

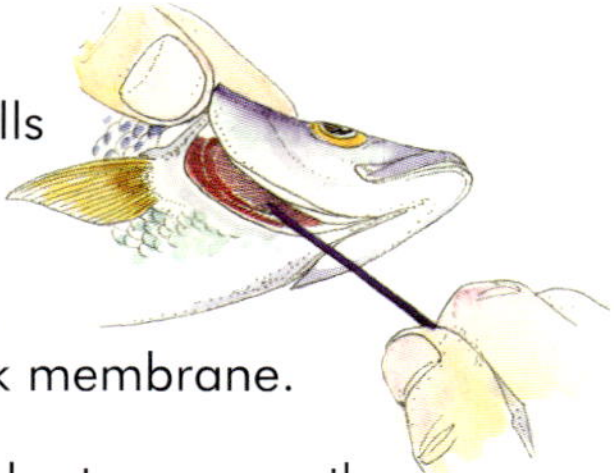

2 Use a metal tube to remove the spine. Enter through the gill area and twist the tube along as it goes to cut the ribs.

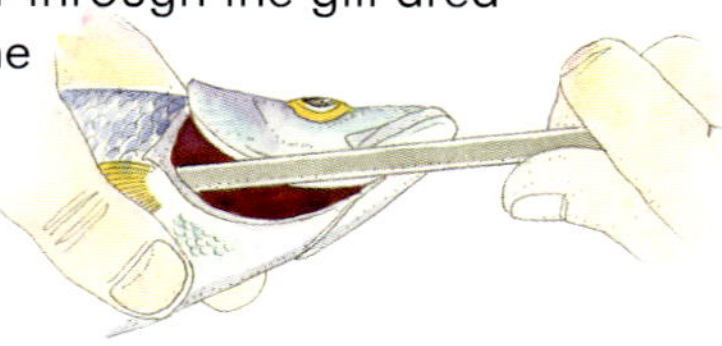

3 Insert the hook by making a small puncture just behind the breast bone.

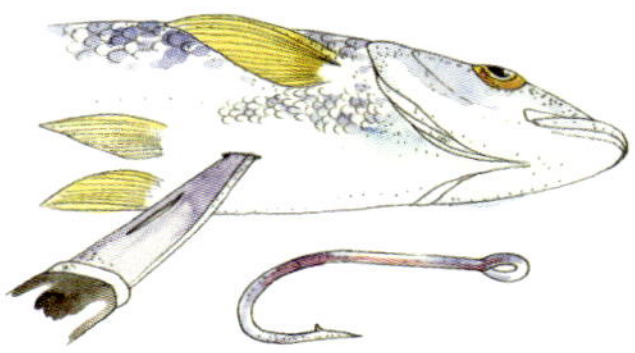

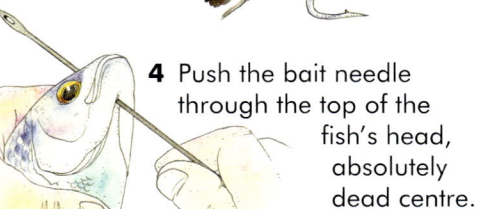

4 Push the bait needle through the top of the fish's head, absolutely dead centre.

5 Align the hook eye with the head puncture hole and push the trace through. Make certain the trace has gone through the eye of the hook.

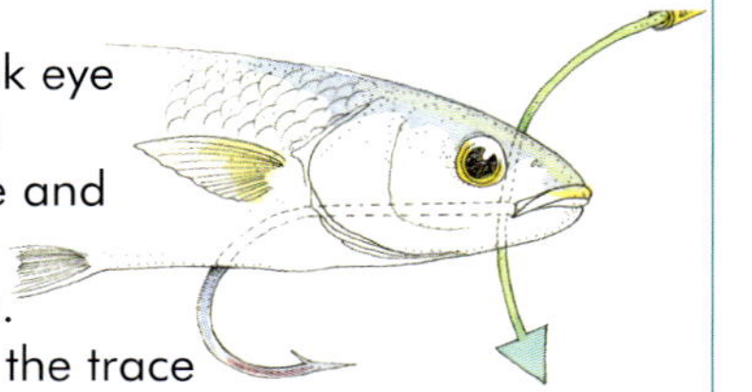

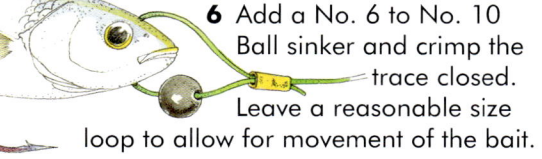

6 Add a No. 6 to No. 10 Ball sinker and crimp the trace closed. Leave a reasonable size loop to allow for movement of the bait.

7 Sew the mouth and gills closed with thread or dental floss.

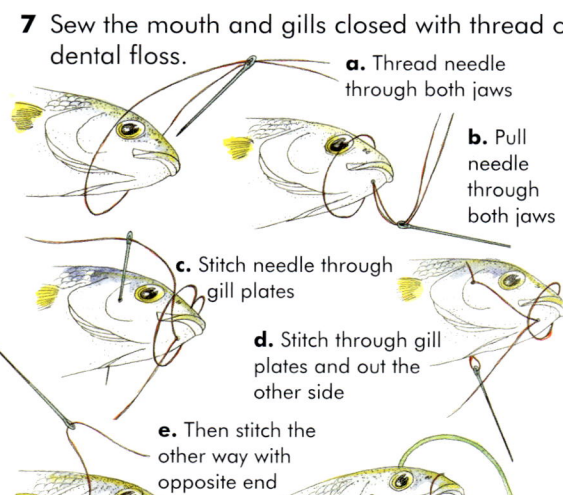

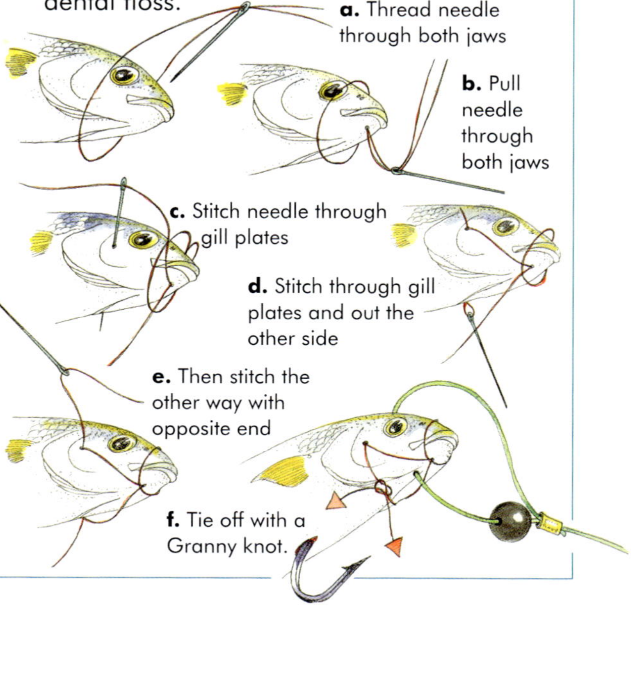

a. Thread needle through both jaws

b. Pull needle through both jaws

c. Stitch needle through gill plates

d. Stitch through gill plates and out the other side

e. Then stitch the other way with opposite end

f. Tie off with a Granny knot.

# RIG 5

## CAIRNS MARLIN RIG

The Cairns marlin rig is a variation on swimming bait rigs used around the world. The change in Cairns is the size of the baits and the fish they catch.

The rig mostly uses .032 or .036 galvanised wire but 400 lb or 600 lb nylon leaders are also used.

The favoured baits are scad or school mackerel but any bait fish can be rigged this way.

The baits work best fished from an outrigger with a long drop back.

### Steps

1. Choose a suitable size fish for bait and remove the backbone with a coring device.

2. Make a pilot hole in the middle of the top of the fish's head for the leader. Then select a hook which is large enough to protrude from behind the breast bone with the eye of the hook in the head of the bait fish.

3. Having made a puncture in the belly of your bait and inserted the hook, thread the leader down through the pilot hole you made in the head, making sure it goes through the eye of the hook. Should you chose to make your bait 'swim' rather than skip, thread a Ball sinker (size 7 to size 10 depending on bait size) onto the leader.

4. Secure your bait on a loop of leader, large enough to allow the bait free movement. Use either the Haywire Twist and Barrel Roll configuration shown here for single strand wire, or a crimped sleeve for monofilament or multi-strand wire.

5. Stitch up the mouth and gills of the bait so it won't fill with water and break up while trolling.
   Double your stitching thread and thread your needle with the loop. Extend the loop and pass it over the nose of the bait fish. Then drive the needle down through both jaws so that the point emerges ahead of the loop.

6. Pull the needle right through together with both tag ends.

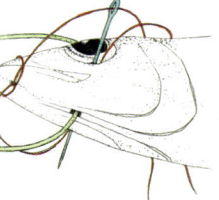

7. Thread your needle with each tag in turn and make a stitch through the eye tunnel of the bait fish, then from the other so that the tags cross in the eye tunnel of the bait fish.

8. Tie the tags off with a Granny knot just behind where the leader emerges under the fish's head. This allows the stitch to be slipped up really tight without unlocking.

9. Make an additional cross stitch through the gill cover, first from one side, then from the other so the tags cross over as before.

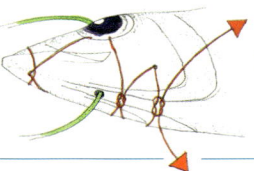

10. Tie off with a Granny knot and the bait is ready to troll.

TROLLING BAITS    63

## RIG 6

# STINGER RIG

This rig is used on either nylon or wire depending on whether the target involves mackerel. The razor lined jaws of the mackerel demand wire.

The rigs are pre-made usually on brown coloured .022 single strand wire or 20 to 30 kg (40 to 60 lb) brown coloured multi-strand wire or 30 to 100 kg (60 to 200 lb) nylon.

This bait is trolled with the reel in gear and the drag firmly set. The aim is to hook the fish as soon as it grabs the bait.

**Steps**

1 A trace of about 1.2 metres (4 ft) is cut and joined to a 4/0 9175 hook.

2 Then a second hook is linked to the eye of the first hook by a short length of wire. The second hook sits down along the back of the bait. Choose a super sharp chemically sharpened hook as the second hook.

3 The lead or nose hook goes in first, side to side through the bait's nose.

4 The second hook carries no weight and is set purely to hook the attacking fish. This hook is set just through the skin to hold it in place and to keep injury to the bait to an absolute minimum.

## RIG 7

# LIVE BAIT TROLLING

Towing live baits is a proven method of catching big fish. Marlin, sailfish, tuna, dolphin fish (mahi mahi), yellowtail kingfish, cobia, mackerel, sharks and others will all fall for a trolled live bait. Baits like large slimy mackerel, large yellowtail, frigate mackerel, cowanyoung and striped tuna (skipjack) all work.

Historically, these baits were rigged using a bridle made of dacron or other strong thread which was tied to the hook and then passed through the eye socket or nose of the bait and was then looped back onto the hook and the bait dropped into the water. This remains a popular and effective method.

The quickest method of rigging these baits is to use a plastic electrical tie.

Live baits are usually trolled with the reel just in gear, with enough drag to stop an overrun when the hit comes and the predator fish is given time and line while it swallows the bait. Once the big fish is presumed to have swallowed the bait the fish is struck and the fight is on.

When a quick rig is required to troll a bait the simple answer is to hook the bait through the nose, side to side.

This rig works perfectly well, but the baits don't last as long, though they last an hour or more which can be plenty. They can also be ripped off the hook at the strike, though this is rare and applies mostly to slimy mackerel.

**Steps**

1 The tie is cut at 45 degrees to give it a sharp point.

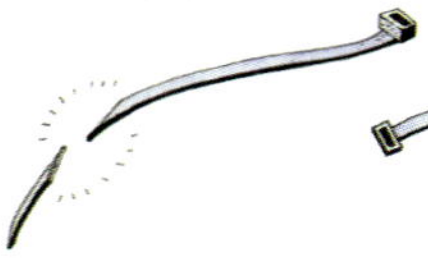

2 Pass the tie through the top of the bait's eye socket and then close it and pull tight.

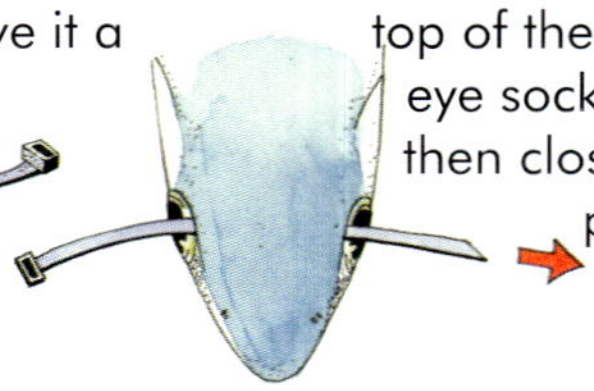

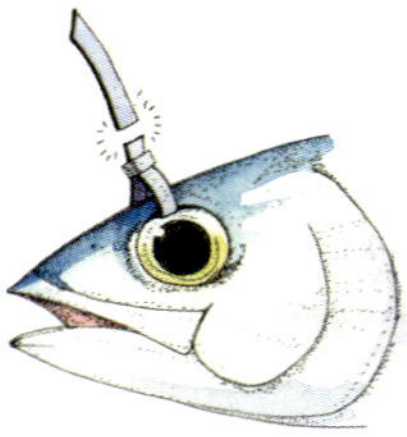

3 Once tight, snip off the tag end.

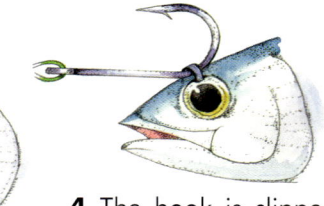

4 The hook is slipped under the tie and the bait is ready to troll.

TROLLING BAITS      65

### RIG 8

# LIVE BAIT TROLLING FOR MARLIN

The rig requires a game fishing outfit rigged with a suitable leader and a suitable hook to which a towing bridle is attached. An open-eye baiting needle is required to attach the bait to the hook.

**STEPS**

**1** The bridle is a short length of monofilament or dacron with a sliding noose in each end. Naturally the size of the bridle depends on the size of the baits you will be trolling but a 10 cm (4 ins) bridle tied in 24 kg (50 lb) line is a good starting point.

**2** Use whatever method you wish to tie your sliding noose at each end of the bridle but this configuration is fine. Don't make the bridle too long.

Pull the second loop tight around a pen, pencil or metal tube so that it locks in the open position and will only close under pressure. Should you tie a number of bridles, do this with both loops.

**3** Slip the open-eye baiting needle onto the loop in the bridle.

**4** Having caught a small tuna, frigate mackerel or other suitable size bait, thread the open-eye needle through the eye tunnel drawing the free loop in the bridle with it.

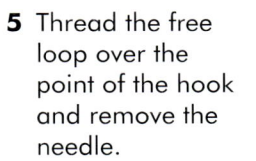

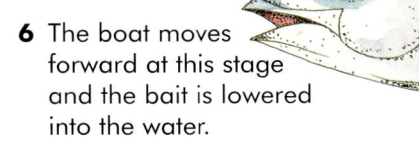

**5** Thread the free loop over the point of the hook and remove the needle.

**6** The boat moves forward at this stage and the bait is lowered into the water.

**7** The boat moves ahead slowly while the angler holds the line. A loop of line is played back into the water behind the boat with the reel on ratchet.

When the angler feels the fish take the bait, release the drop-back. Wait till the line is running off the reel at a constant pace, then engage strike drag.

At this point the boat driver should accelerate the boat forward. Firstly, to assist the angler to hook the fish, secondly to minimise the risk of a lively fish running ahead of the boat.

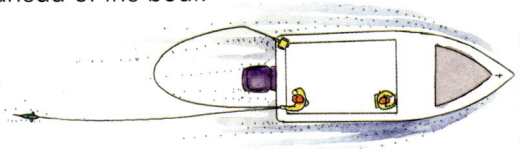

Some migratory fish rely on these annual gatherings and their migratory travels are timed to arrive at the same time and place as the bait fish.

The use of colour and LCD sounders means these bait fish concentrations are often located as the boat moves around the fishing area. They can also be found on the surface.

Often, seabirds will be found circling one patch of ocean without actually landing or feeding. Checking this area will often reveal a school of bait down in the depths. It may be too deep for the birds to feed on but they can see it from above.

Once the bait fish have been located, it may be absolutely obvious that they are under attack just by the commotion in the ocean.

Tuna are messy feeders often blasting the bait fish off the top and becoming airborne themselves.

Other attacks, particularly by billfish are much more subtle and occur at depth and are never seen by anglers.

There are also times when the bait fish are simply being shadowed by their predators and the introduction of a wounded bait fish (on a hook) generates the strike.

## CATCHING THE FISH

In a free-for-all surface feeding situation it may just be a matter of trolling lures around the mayhem to get strikes.

Often though the fish are focused on the target bait and won't strike a lure.

In this situation, if you have live bait, either hook it on through the nose or bridle it and pay it back out. Then use the boat to slow troll it into position.

Sabiki style bait jigs can be used to catch the bait fish if you need some live baits, though this may depend on the level of attack they are under.

When working an area with obvious or easily found bait schools but with no visible predators a change of tactics is needed.

The usual technique is to run baits set so the fish

An effortlessly airborne black marlin gets going after taking a swimming gar.

# Trolling Baits

can attack them. The bait pattern is set with one short, one long and one deep bait on a downrigger.

This arrangement helps prevent, but not stop, one attacking fish from grabbing more than one bait.

The baits can be run from either the rod holder or outriggers depending on personal preference.

A witchdoctor teaser is added to the pattern to draw extra attention to the baits.

With the pattern set, the boat can slowly troll around the bait fish looking for strikes.

The reels are set with just enough drag to prevent an overrun and the fish are allowed to swallow the bait before striking.

One trick where there are numerous bait balls is to watch where the strikes come from. There maybe twenty bait balls in an area but only one or two may have predatory fish around them.

If a marlin comes off one patch it is highly likely another one or more will be on the same patch.

Mark its location on the plotter or keep watch as the hooked fish is played. Once the hooked fish is landed or tagged return and work the same school again.

Slow trolling with live bait does not cover much ground so it is important to keep the boat in the strike zone by staying close to the bait fish for as long as possible.

## DOWNRIGGERS

Downriggers really help when targeting bait balls. If the bait balls are showing on the sounder at 30 metres (90 ft) then the downrigger bait should be set at close to this distance.

It is wise to work only one downrigger to avoid tangles as some tight boat manoeuvres are often needed to keep the baits in the right place or just work in general boat traffic that often congregates in 'hot bite' areas.

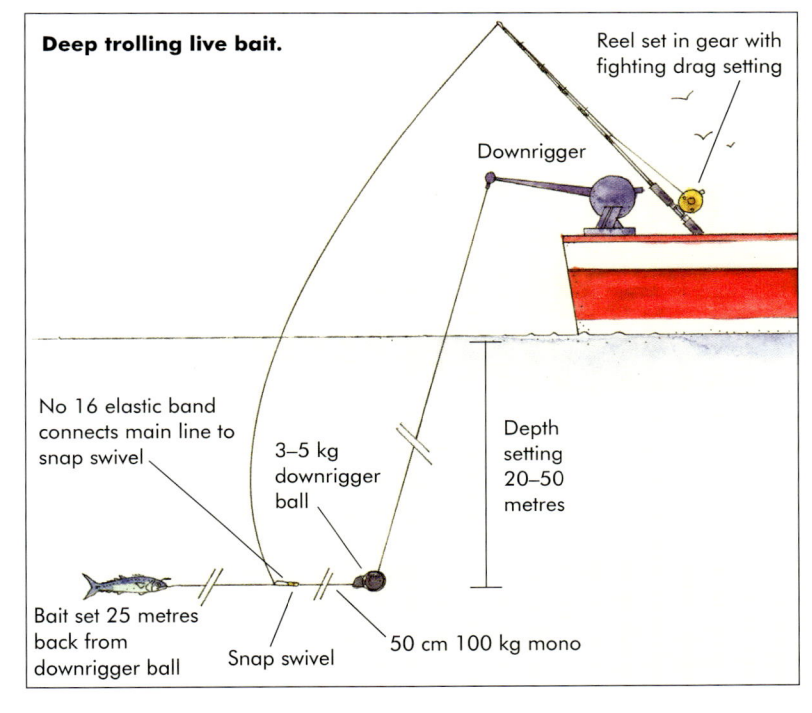

**Deep trolling live bait.**

- Reel set in gear with fighting drag setting
- Downrigger
- No 16 elastic band connects main line to snap swivel
- 3–5 kg downrigger ball
- Depth setting 20–50 metres
- Bait set 25 metres back from downrigger ball
- Snap swivel
- 50 cm 100 kg mono

A tagged mako shark about to be released.
PHOTO: GLEN BOOTH

# CHAPTER 7

# SHARKS

There are few marine creatures that stir the imagination as readily as sharks. They may not be every game fisherman's cup of tea, but they can provide exciting sport.

There are seven varieties of sharks commonly encountered by Australian game fishermen. These are the tiger shark (*Galeocerdo cuvieri*), the great white (*Carcharodon carcharias*), the mako (*Isurus glaucus*), the hammerhead (*Sphyrna spp.*), the blue shark (*Prionace glauca*), thresher (*Alopias vulpinus*) and the whalers (*Carcharhinus spp.*). The great white shark is fully protected in Australian and South African waters.

With the exception of the mako which will jump, none of these is as spectacular as the billfish, but what they lack in speed and acrobatic ability, sharks make up for with sheer bulk and dogged tenacity. Mako, hammerhead and whaler sharks are fast and can run long distances when hooked.

Other than blue sharks very few of the larger varieties ever come easy on rod and reel, and encounters with truly big specimens have been known to go on for hours—even with heavy tackle.

In the temperate and tropical waters, sharks are sometimes considered pests—unwanted intruders that pinch baits intended for other game fish, or that mutilate prized captures during the fight. In the colder waters, however, where game species may be few and far between, the number of specialist shark anglers is on the increase. The relative availability of the larger varieties, both inshore and out wide, makes them welcome adversaries in areas where tuna and billfish are limited in numbers or do not frequent those waters.

## TACKLING SHARKS

Before playing games with a creature that may weigh anything up to a tonne, the first precaution any shark angler should take is to ensure that the boat is suitable for the task.

This means having strong bollards, quality flying gaffs and tail ropes.

## BERLEY (CHUM)

Berley is the key to success when pursuing sharks. It would surprise many people to discover the amount of berley some specialist shark anglers take to sea for a day's fishing. Tuna makes the ideal berley base for sharks in any situation, but other oily fish like mullet and slimy mackerel will do the job.

Transom mounted berley buckets are very effective for distributing an enticing chum slick. Berley buckets are a great device for laying down a trail irresistible to marauding sharks. Once located by the shark, its

*A blue shark makes a B line for a fillet of striped tuna set in the berley trail.*

incredible sense of smell will guide it along the trail and up to the boat.

## BAITING UP

Whole or filleted tuna, salmon, mullet, bonito or other oily fish are the most commonly used shark baits. A whole fish of between 2 or 3 kg (4 or 6 lb) is spot on for larger sharks. Smaller baits are matched to smaller sharks depending on what may come up the berley trail.

## TACKLE NEEDS

Terminal tackle needed to take on large sharks must be robust and well constructed. Under IGFA rules, the maximum wire trace permissible is 30 feet and it's a good idea to use every inch of this when specialising in tigers and makos. These sharks are notorious for rolling, jumping and other troublesome antics when hooked, and long wire traces are needed to keep their sandpaper like skins and razor sharp teeth away from fragile mono line. On smaller sharks, lighter traces around 3 to 4 metres (9 to 12 ft) work well.

Mustad Seamasters (7699) are by far the most popular choice in shark hooks, as they are tremendously strong and maintain a good point. Any large, strong hook will work, the hook choice is very much up to the angler.

*A big 220 kg tiger hangs from the weigh station. Fish like this are never captured easily.*

*A small mako shows how aggressive the species can be by attacking a striped tuna that was being caught for bait.*

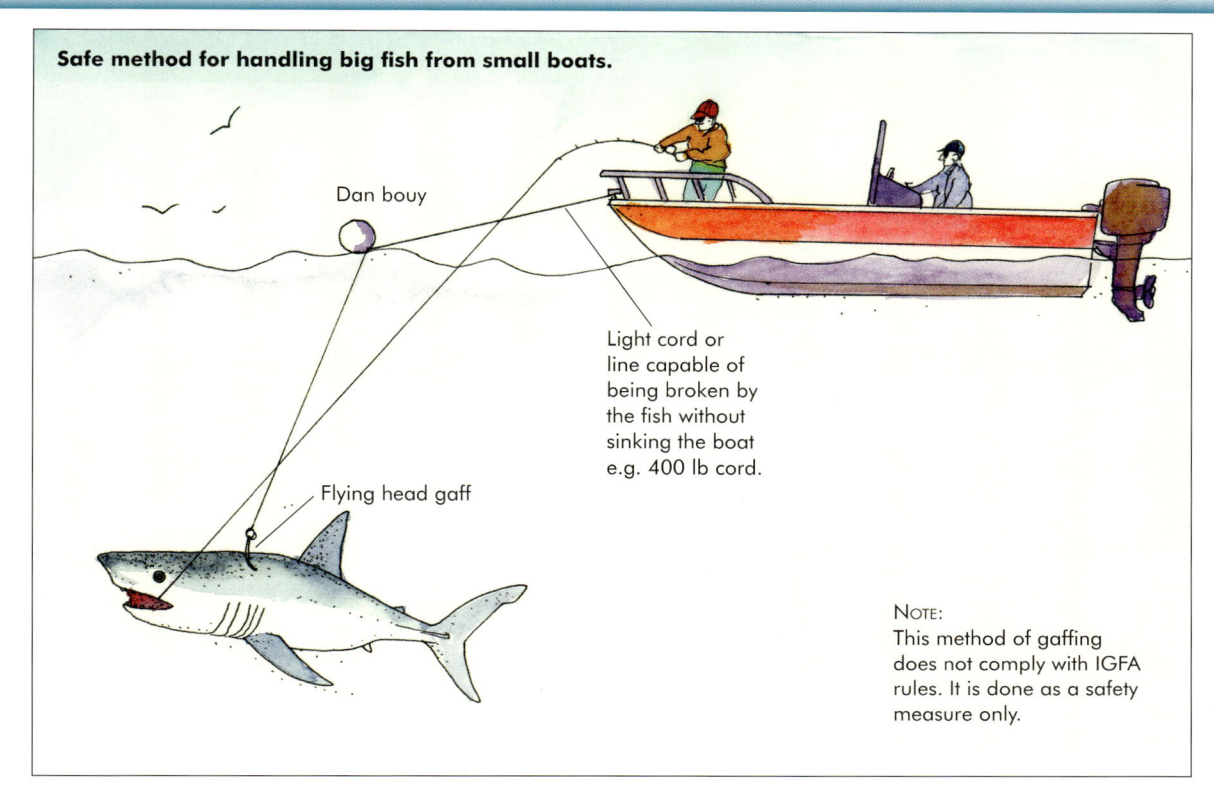

### Safe method for handling big fish from small boats.

- Dan bouy
- Light cord or line capable of being broken by the fish without sinking the boat e.g. 400 lb cord.
- Flying head gaff

NOTE: This method of gaffing does not comply with IGFA rules. It is done as a safety measure only.

For sharks from 50 to 200 kg (100 to 400 lb), hooks in the 8/0 to 12/0 range are sufficient, but when you are looking at heavy weights, hook sizes need to be upgraded. On larger sharks hooks up to 20/0 may be used particularly if big baits are being presented. The aim is to balance the hook size and trace strength to match the size shark expected to be hooked, and the weight of tackle being employed.

Quality lever drag game reels and powerful rods are the most suitable tools for bulky sharks. High quality harnesses and rod buckets or fighting chairs are an advantage when handling large sharks.

## GAFFING

Just about all the large species mentioned, with the possible exception of the blue shark, have reputations at the gaff. Large sharks are notorious for rolling wildly when the flyer goes in, and this is where small boats and inexperienced crews can become a dangerous combination. On small boats, secure the flying gaff to a dan buoy or foam float to avoid capsize or swamping if things go wrong. The shark is allowed to drag the float overboard if things get too wild.

## TAKE OR TAG

Hanging a big shark on a weigh station is still done in fishing tournaments but many anglers are just as happy to take a photo and release their fish.

It depends on the situation and what is happening with the disposal of the captured fish.

*A small hammerhead lets rip on the gaff.*

Spanish mackerel are about the largest species encountered when trolling inshore.
PHOTO: DAVID ROCHE

# CHAPTER 8

# INSHORE TROLLING

Inshore trolling targets many of the more coastal sportfish found closer to the shore and offshore reef systems. These fish include some of our most popular sportfish like yellowtail kingfish, Spanish mackerel, cobia, trevally, tailor, salmon, longtail tuna, mackerel tuna, bonito, coral trout and many others.

In fact the list of fish possible is impressive and the technique is invaluable for small boats working the popular and hard fished inshore coastal areas.

While this chapter is based on trolling, working inshore areas is usually more wholistic with a bit of lurecasting and live baiting thrown into an average day to maximise results.

This technique produces fish in both temperate and tropical seas, only the fish species change and kelp is replaced by coral when the water gets warmer.

## MINNOW LURES

Minnow type lures are the main platform used by inshore trollers. Their swimming action and flexibility to work at speeds from 3 to 12 knots makes them a very reliable fish producer.

The lures are usually selected to match the bait

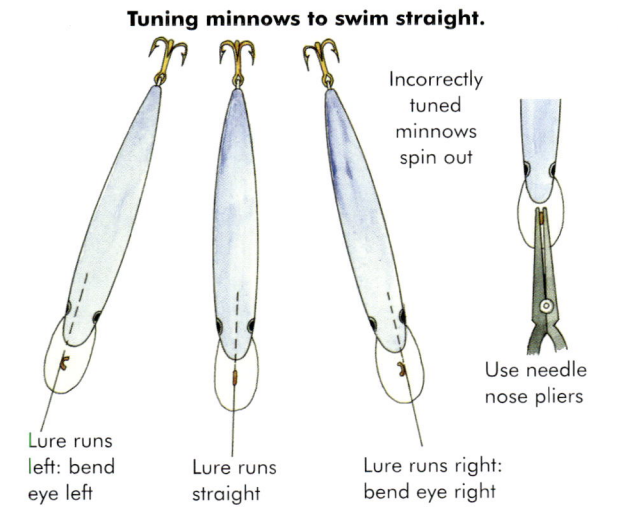

*Offshore coral islands and reefs are likely fish producers.*

**Tuning minnows to swim straight.**

Incorrectly tuned minnows spin out

Use needle nose pliers

Lure runs left: bend eye left

Lure runs straight

Lure runs right: bend eye right

fish in an area and the type of fish being chased. In general this means smaller lures from 9 to 14 cm (4 to 6 ins) for smaller fish and larger lures from 15 to 25 cm (6 to 10ins) for the bigger fish.

Lure choice is a matter of personal preference, and so long as the lure has a good bait fish shape and will swim at a range of trolling speeds it will catch fish.

Lures having either the traditional minnow shape or bibless minnows will work.

The most important point is to check the lures are fitted with extra strong hooks and rings and the lures are 'tuned' to swim straight and not weaving out to one side or 'blowing' out of the water.

This jumping or blowing out can be a frustrating part of working with minnows. They are great fish catcher but they can be knocked out or pulled out of tune, this stops them working effectively.

This tune or straight running can be restored by using a pair of pliers and gently bending the towing eye back towards the side of the lure that runs deeper in the water.

The best lure colours are red and white, light blue, pink, silver, green and orange.

The lures are usually rigged on one metre of 25 to 30 kg (50 to 60 lb) nylon trace with a black swivel to connect to the main line and a light but strong black snap swivel to connect to the lure. In tropical and warmer temperate waters where mackerel and other toothy fish live, 30 kg (60 lb) wire is used to protect the lure from being bitten off.

Minnows are not the only lures which work on inshore sportfish. Small skirted lures with metal or plastic heads or squid type trolling lures also take a wide range of fish.

Specialised high speed trolling lures are used when trolling inshore for mackerel species. These lures are towed well behind the boat around 70 to 100 metres (210 to 300 ft) and at speeds of 10 to 15 knots.

The technique is highly successful and produces very good catches of mackerel. Lures like the Wilson No. 2 Sea Jet and hex head type lures form the basis of this fishing style.

These lures are often trolled in combination with minnow lures to give the fish a wider selection of food targets. Rigging of the lures is shown in the Catching Light Game Fish section.

## FINDING THE FISH

Most of the inshore sports fish use the underwater geography as hunting grounds or places to hold when attacking bait fish. Deep headlands, shallow reefs surrounded by deeper water, offshore islands, bommies with breaking wash, channels between reefs and islands, the base of cliffs and anywhere that holds

LEFT: Giant trevally are a great test of both gear and angler.

BELOW: Trevally regularly school around drop offs and bommies.

Spanish mackerel are probably the fastest and most aggressive of the inshore sportfish.

concentrations of bait fish are all worth checking.

Always look for current movement around many of these places as water movement is often very important in positioning both bait fish and the feeding activity of the bigger fish. Wherever the current strikes a bommie, coral, rock, headland, island or whatever is always going to be a likely fish producer.

A good knowledge of the fishing area and the more productive spots is a big help in finding the fish but this technique is also handy for those visiting an area to search for good fish.

Many of the spots can be found on marine charts of an area. The islands, reefs and shallow areas will all be marked and will give the angler a good guide to the underwater geography.

## TACKLE

Relatively light tackle can be used for most of the inshore sportfish, although fish like yellowtail kingfish, coral trout, magnum trevally and cobia can make life difficult and even expensive at times.

Where tough fish are expected, equally tough tackle may be needed. This usually means 15 kg line on a medium to large overhead reel and a matching fast tapered rod.

A large baitcaster or medium overhead reel filled with 6 to 10 kg (12 to 20 lb) line is used in most situations. Medium to large threadlines can also be used. This type of fishing is about having fun and enjoying the fish and suits a light approach. If a particularly large fish gets in on the act then the angler does their best to land it, it's part of the challenge.

When large inshore predators are regularly encountered a switch to 25 kg (50 lb) braided lines and correspondingly heavy traces can be used to counter their fierce power dives and passion for breaking anglers off on the bottom or the coral.

# TECHNIQUE

Early morning is usually the best time for this type of fishing, with most of the action over by 9 or 10 am. Being on the water as the sun comes up is important when working inshore areas.

Lure choices are made to relate to known target species in most areas. This depends a little on experience and the fish species expected. In most cases, the more common fish will be targeted and anything else that comes along will be a bonus.

Usually four lures are set, two at 20 to 25 metres (60 to 75 ft) off the stern and two at 35 to 40 metres (105 to 120 ft) back. A mixture of minnow and small skirted lures are trolled although lure selection may vary depending on the fish being chased.

Where the boat is being manoeuvred through tight spaces or in spots where big fish are expected, only two outfits may be trolled to allow for the handling of the fish, gear and the boat.

Much of the fishing is done at relatively close range to breaking seas and areas where shallow water falls rapidly into deep water.

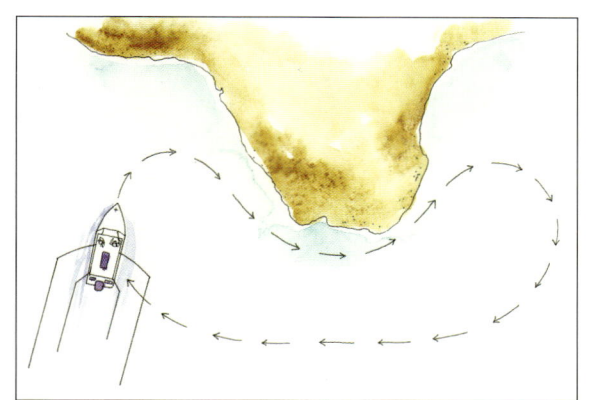

**Trolling pattern for inshore species.**

Lures set as matched pairs to allow tight turns near fish or structures.

Squid type lures set at 20–25 metres

Minnow lures set at 30–40 metres

Suggested trolling pattern for working a headland, reef or island edge.

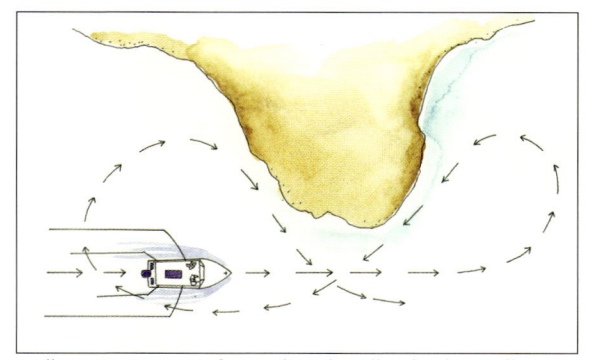

Trolling pattern No.2 for working headlands, drop-offs and corners of islands.

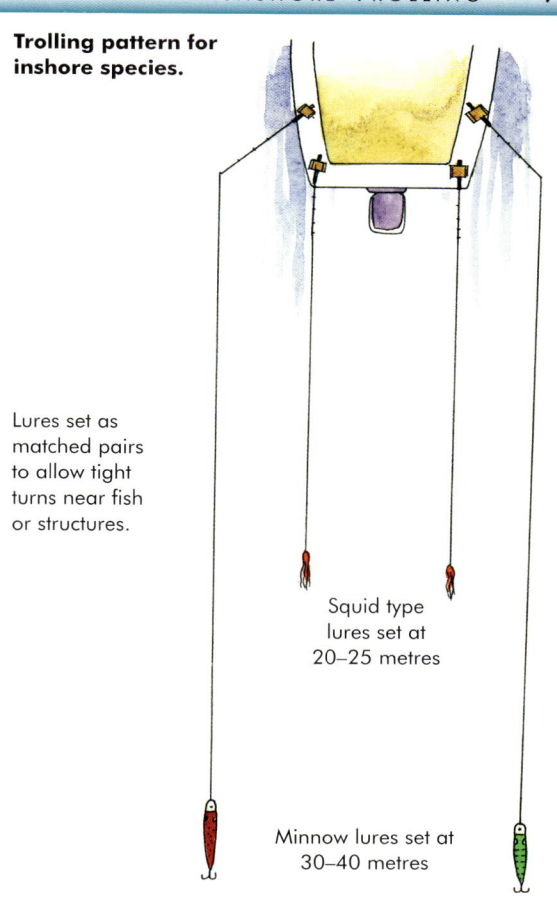

The skipper needs to be alert to the dangers of such places and keep the boat in safe water. This often means someone stays on the wheel at all times.

It is also possible to track the lures into the right spots by turning the boat to provide angles across the face of drop offs or near bommies or breaking water.

The boat is an important tool in the whole game of inshore trolling.

Boat speed should be from 4 to 7 knots for general fishing although mackerel and the tuna species are often more interested in lures trolled at higher speeds up to 15 knots.

The more open water inshore predators like tuna and several others can often be found schooling on the surface, with birds diving and wheeling on the bait fish.

These fish can be trolled but often more success will be had casting to the schools using metal lures and then retrieving them quickly through the school.

Inshore trolling is often highly productive on a wide range of sport and table fish. Just remember when the fish are thick to keep enough for a feed and let the rest go.

A big, bruising giant trevally caught on a big popper.
PHOTO: GLEN BOOTH

# CHAPTER 9

# LURE CASTING

Lure casting is one of the most exciting forms of bluewater fishing. The fishing is very visual, lures arc through the air in the direction of the feeding fish, anglers arms crank hard and the lure disappears in a spectacular surface strike.

The hard work starts once the fish is hooked and it is played to the boat.

Lure casting is a universally popular angling technique and works whether the anglers are at Bermagui or Bermuda.

The aim is to present a lure by casting and then provide the lure with the right action and retrieve speed to be hit by the feeding fish.

There are two main forms of lure casting, one is to open water species and the other is to places like coral bommies, rocky outcrops, shallow reefs and similar places where predatory fish are likely to be holding.

## OPEN WATER

Schools of fish are regularly found attacking bait in open water. These schools may be tuna, mackerel, trevally, queenfish, salmon, tailor, yellowtail kingfish or whatever, depending on the area being fished.

The presence of the feeding fish is often signposted by seabirds grouped together wheeling and diving on the bait fish being attacked from below. Sometimes the schools of feeding fish just erupt in the fishing

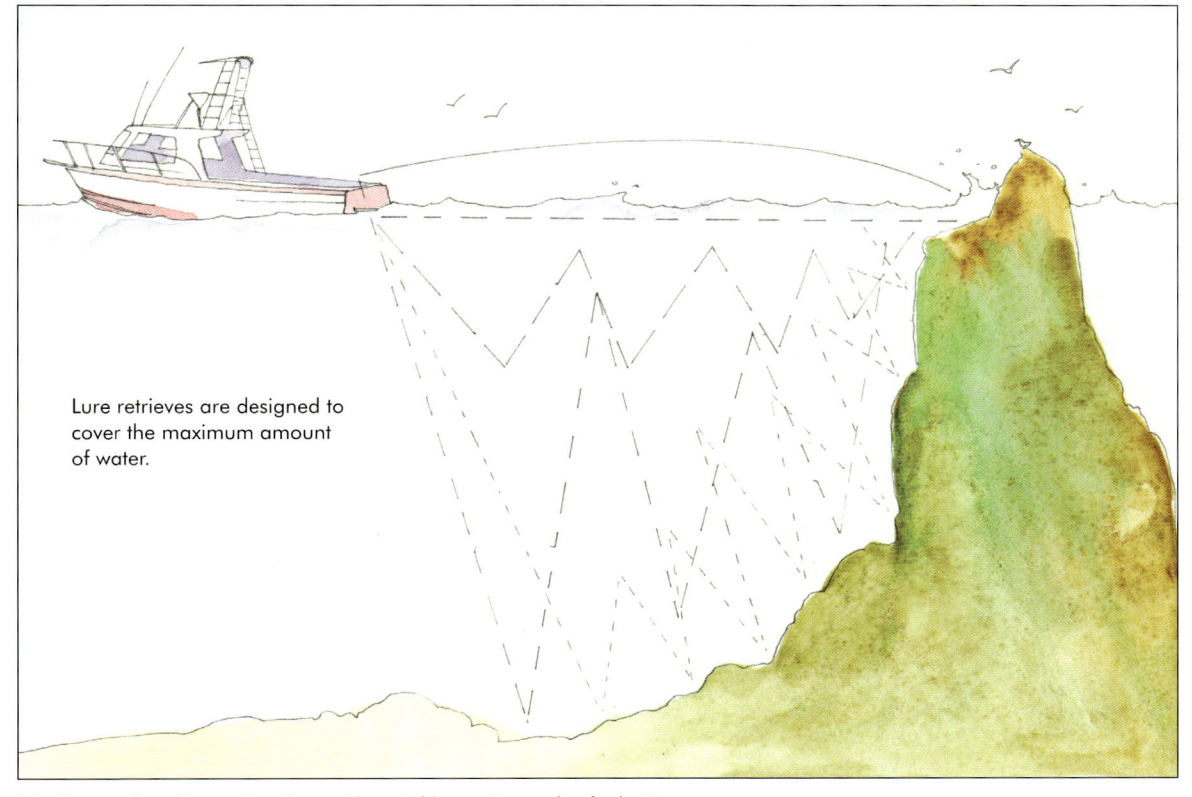

Lure retrieves are designed to cover the maximum amount of water.

Working reef and bommie edges with metal lures, jigs and soft plastics.

area and may not have any birds with them at all.

Anglers can then cast a lure, usually a metal slice or bait fish imitation across or near the feeding fish and then bring the lure quickly through the feeding mass of fish. Other lures like minnows or poppers can also be used depending on the species involved.

The result often comes with a solid strike and a hooked fish to be played out. The gear is generally light to facilitate the easy casting of the lures so most of the fish get a chance to display their power.

In open water there are few threats, the fish generally can't reef the angler and so long as an appropriate trace is used the fish just needs to be fought to the boat.

Open water lure casting can also be effective while drifting or at anchor, because it will pick up an odd passing fish and passes the time productively.

## AREA SPECIFIC CASTING

There are places in the ocean that just naturally hold big fish. These are the spots where they hold and feed on the surrounding bait fish population.

The best spots are shallow reefs surrounded by deeper water, the edges of deep headlands, drop offs, rocky outcrops, offshore islands or places where ocean currents meet some kind of obstruction, or run between reefs or islands.

It does not matter whether it is a warm coral reef or a kelp covered reef in cold country, if conditions are right the fish will feed there. It may be mackerel, trevally and coral trout in the tropics or yellowtail kingfish, barracouta, snook, tailor and salmon in temperate areas but the technique changes little.

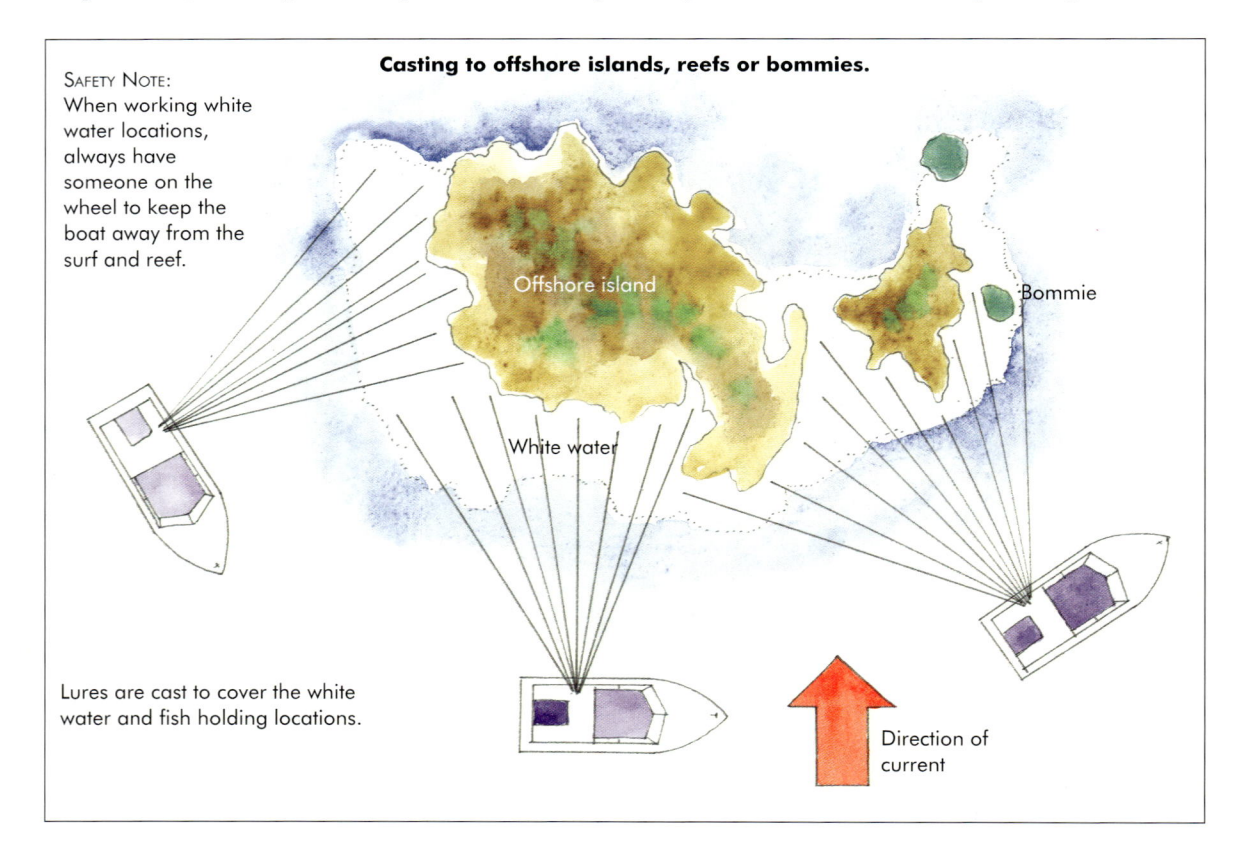

*Keep someone on the wheel at all times when working close to the active surf zone.*

**Casting to offshore islands, reefs or bommies.**

SAFETY NOTE: When working white water locations, always have someone on the wheel to keep the boat away from the surf and reef.

Lures are cast to cover the white water and fish holding locations.

Offshore island
Bommie
White water
Direction of current

Again metal lures work well because of their casting qualities. The lures enable the boat to stand off perhaps otherwise dangerous locations and allows the anglers to fire the lures at the right spot.

Poppers are often extremely effective in these locations with their wounded, splashing and spluttering action drawing strikes from a wide range of fish.

Some fish though are genuinely excited by poppers with trevally, cobia, mackerel and queenfish in the tropics and yellowtail kingfish, tailor and salmon in the temperate zone being the main targets.

Working lures around hard reef country is not without its difficulties. Lures allowed to sink too deeply will often be snagged and lost. The fish too will use the rugged underwater geography to their advantage looking for places to cut the angler off. Some fish like coral trout and yellowtail kingfish are experts at reefing the angler, often in quick time.

It makes for fun fishing with moments of high drama and often very difficult but highly rewarding fights.

*A metal lure and a good casting outfit can be used to take a wide variety of fish.*

*Mackerel tuna taken on a bait fish profile type lure.*

## TACKLE

The casting qualities of the tackle are very important and both rod and reel need to be a good marriage to work well.

A 2 metre (6–7 ft) light tipped fast tapered rod with the reel seat mounted for double handed casting is the preferred weapon.

The reel can be either a medium to large threadline or a large baitcaster or overhead type reel. The important part about the reel is that it must have a high gear ratio to get the lures moving at the speed many of the target fish feed. This is particularly important when casting metal lures at tuna and mackerel, but not so important when working around the washes and reefs. Whichever reel is chosen the angler needs to be comfortable casting with it, so threadlines are often the best choice rather than overheads. The reel also needs to be strongly engineered and have a smooth, premium quality drag.

## LURES

The metal lures are usually 60 to 90 gram slices or moulded fish shaped lures. These lures use a

*A solid yellowtail kingfish is worked to the boat.*

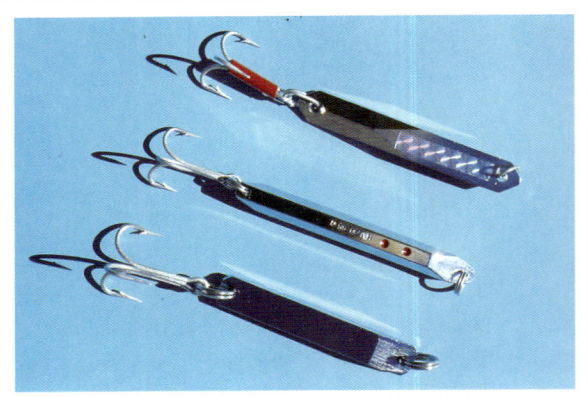

*Sliced metal bar type lures are very popular with lure casters.*

*Moulded baitfish profiles provide an obvious attraction to aggressive fish.*

combination of speed and basic bait fish profile to draw strikes from the target species. The best colours are either chromed or painted white or pink.

## POPPERS

One of the most spectacular forms of lure casting is fishing with poppers.

The whole process is visual, with the lure arcing out across the sea, then chugging, splooshing, spluttering and skipping across the surface back to the boat.

As the lure comes back the fish attack with massive surface strikes, engulfing the lure sending spray everywhere. The fish are often seen as they follow and attack the lure.

When the line comes tight at the hook-up these big reef dwellers take off at high speed trying to bury the angler in the bottom.

In years gone by, this combat was done with

*Giant trevally taken from a coral bommie on a popper, classical tropical fishing.*

*It is easy to smile when you have caught a big kingfish like this on a popper. In shallow water these are the toughest fish that swim.*

large threadlines or medium overhead reels and with castable size nylon line up to around 15 kg (30 lb). The big yellowtail kingfish, cobia, giant trevally, and amberjacks often won. Sometimes they were next to impossible to catch on conventional tackle.

The development of high strength threadlines like the Shimano Stella and Diawa Saltiga combined with braided lines now means these bar room brawls are far more even.

These reels can cope with 25 kg (50 lb) or even 40 kg (80 lb) braid and can work with drag loadings of 15 kg (30 lb) and more.

When working at these drag levels this is not a sport for the inexperienced. The new technology though does put the angler in a much more competitive position when working in difficult terrain.

The leaders used are usually 100 kg (200 lb) mono or wire and matching heavy walled but light tipped rods are used for casting and taking the huge weight loading applied in this form of fishing.

The same high strength threadlines are also being used to cast baits to marlin and tuna feeding or swimming on the surface.

It is a useful, if rather expensive, development in tackle that offers some new options for bluewater anglers.

Poppers are a matter of personal choice although some work far better than others. A little trial and error is often needed to find the type the local fish are interested in.

Where larger fish like great trevally, yellowtail kingfish and coral dwellers are chased, the lures need extra strong hooks and split rings to hold the fish.

## RIGGING

Rigging casting lures is easy, with half a metre or a little less of 30 kg (60 lb) nylon linked to the main line by a black swivel being the standard. Where mackerel, coral trout and barracuda are an issue, the same length of 30 kg (60 lb) multi-strand wire will help minimise bite-offs.

## BOAT HANDLING

Some boat handling skills are necessary for successful bluewater lure casting.

When working around schools of feeding fish it is important to not rush up and scare them with the boat. Move up to the fish at an easy non threatening speed.

Don't get too close, use the available casting distance of the tackle to stand off and work the school.

Use the wind, if possible, to add casting distance and allow the wind to drift the boat in the direction of the feeding fish with the motor off.

Always remember the boat casts a shadow and has a shape that feeding fish relate to large sharks or whales. If the schools are 'spooked' by the boat work with the sun in your face, this will throw the shadow away from the fish.

When casting around rocks, bommies and near active surf zones one angler should stay on the wheel at all times. The waves, wind and currents can place the boat in danger if someone does not keep watch over what is happening.

Lure casting close to headlands, islands and bommies is an active and productive fishing method.

Big cobia are a real challenge on saltwater fly tackle.
PHOTO: BILL CLASSON

# CHAPTER 10

# SALTWATER FLY FISHING

Saltwater fly fishing has been a growing part of offshore angling over the past decade.

In many ways, saltwater fly fishing is like lure casting except the fly is cast by the fly line rather than by the weight of the lure. The same tactics and techniques that work for lure casting work equally well using saltwater fly.

The reason for the popularity of fly fishing relates to the challenge involved. The craft needs a bit of work and the fish caught provide an enjoyable fight.

## FISH TAKER

Anglers who have not seen saltwater flies in action may be surprised to see how keen some species of fish are to nail the fly.

Most surface feeding school fish are relatively easy to catch on fly with fish like yellowtail kingfish, trevally, queenfish, dolphin fish (mahi mahi) and most tuna being highly attracted.

Some anglers have taken the challenge side of fly fishing to the extreme and regularly catch marlin using the fly. Other big fish like mako sharks, cobia and yellowfin tuna are also taken on the long wand.

## NOT TROUT

Fly fishing is historically based on trout fishing where the insect imitations are cast to the insect eating trout.

Saltwater fliers are tied to imitate bait fish and are cast in traditional fly casting manner. Once the fly hits the water it is not left static, it is retrieved by hand, called stripping, back to the boat.

The retrieve can be quite fast and gives the fly an enticing dart and pulse action which fish find highly attractive.

## TACKLE

Saltwater fly tackle is designed to handle big, fast fish and most reels have good drags and anti-reverse systems. The reels are not cheap either but they do a good job. The reels are designed to hold the complete fly line and 500 metres (1500 ft) of backing.

As with trout rods, the rods used in saltwater fly are rated to the weight fly lines they were designed to cast.

Most SWF enthusiasts use size 10, 11 or 12 lines and rods and leaders from 6 to 15 kg (12 to 30 lb). The size fly outfit used is a matter of personal choice and many anglers fish for smaller sportfish on lighter line just for fun, using basic trout gear most of the time.

As the popularity of saltwater fly fishing continues to grow the sight of long rods and gliding fly line will become a regular part of bluewater angling.

For those looking to do something challenging and different saltwater fly has much to offer

A brace of kingfish caught on a small popper.

All sorts of fish will take deepwater jigs, big and small it can be a lottery.
PHOTO: DAVID ROCHE

# CHAPTER 11

# JIGGING

Jigging is a style of fishing which relies on a metal lure being dropped to the sea bed or into the depths and worked either up or down or back to the boat in a matter that imitates a bait fish.

In many ways it is just another form of lure casting where the lure is worked vertically instead of horizontally but there is a little more to it than just retrieving a lure.

Jigging has two basic forms, one uses a heavy metal lure which can be shaped to provide action or be fairly straight and relies on speed for its attraction.

The second part of jigging uses a lead head jig with a tail made of various fibres or tinsel. The jig head carries the hook in an upright position to minimise the chance of snagging the bottom and maximise the fish holding quality of the lure.

The lead head jigs are designed predominantly to catch bottom fish while the metal jigs are aimed at reef and oceanic predators like yellowtail kingfish, cobia, tuna, trevally and mackerel.

*An inshore jigging combination, quality threadline, 120 gram jig and a solid kingfish.*

## GEAR FOR JIGGING

Jigging has traditionally been done with highly geared overhead reels and fast tapered, light tipped rods.

This style of fishing has changed over time and now quality threadlines are being used very specifically for jigging.

These highly developed threadlines can also deliver extremely powerful drag loadings and stiffer rods with much less tip action have been developed to match them.

Braided line has also added a significant new level to jigging. Braid allows for deeper water to be fished and its non stretch qualities mean more action can be added to the lure.

Finally, the jigs themselves have had a significant development with 'knife' or 'blade' jigs adding a new dimension to the sport.

These long, thin but heavy jigs have a strong single hook spliced to the top eyelet of the lure. It is a Japanese development and it is devastatingly effective.

All these developments have led to a resurgence in jigging.

## TRADITIONAL JIGS

Traditional jigs are heavy metal lures either molded or shaped to provide a swimming action or cut lengths of metal rod that were chromed or coloured.

These lures were dropped to the bottom and then retrieved, usually at speed, to the surface or half way back or whatever.

Apart from the retrieve speed, extra action was imparted to the lure with a rhythmical lift and drop of the rod. This gave the lure a pulsating, darting action.

## BLADE JIGS

Blade jigs are a development of the traditional jigs with a lot of thought added.

The long jigs are heavy, weighing from 250 grams to 500 grams (½ to 1 lb) and are designed to be fished in deep water.

They are long and thin in profile with their unique hook mounting system at the head of the jig.

Blade jigs are also fished a little differently to conventional jigs. They are lifted and flicked off the bottom or at the working depth with exaggerated rod lifts and are often taken as they flutter back down.

These exaggerated lifts and drops are done four or five times, lifting the jig through 30 metres (90 ft) or so and then repeated.

Their large, single hooks give them excellent fish holding power which is needed as many anglers are combining them with 25 to 40 kg (50 to 80 lb) braid and fishing with 10 to 14 kgs (20 to 28 lb) or more of drag.

It is a brutal exercise, but on big fish it adds a new element to jigging.

## LEAD HEAD JIGS

Lead head jigs are mostly used to target reef fish but will work right across the jigging spectrum.

As the name suggests they are made up with a heavy lead head then a tail of feathers, fibre or flash to imitate a bait fish or squid.

On reef fish the jigs can also be 'sweetened' with strips of flesh, squid tentacles or squid heads to make the lure more appealing to the target fish.

The jigs feature an upturned hook which helps to snag proof them around rock and coral.

When worked with a lift and drop technique combined with a slow retrieve these lures have a high

ABOVE: Traditional jig top and bottom with blade jig in the middle.

ABOVE: Kingfish with 120 gram rig.

Spanish mackerel are very regularly taken on jigs around the warmer reefs.

A solid king comes to the boat taken on a large sliced metal lure.

success rate on snapper, sweetlip, emperor, cod, coral trout, trevally and other aggressive reef fish.

When worked with faster retrieves they will also take yellowtail kingfish, amberjack and tuna.

## SOFT PLASTICS

Traditional jig heads can also be fitted with a range of lifelike soft plastic tails to tempt all manner of reef fish.

Snapper, cod, sweetlips, trevally, mulloway, yellowtail kingfish and cobia are all tempted by these lifelike jigs.

The size jig head used varies depending on the water depth. Many of these jigs are fished on light heads in shallow water and are twitched and flicked rather than bounced around in more traditional styles.

They will work just as well on heavily weighted heads bounced around the deep reefs.

These soft plastic lures are very lifelike and have great appeal to the fish. They are fun to fish with and catch a lot of fish when used in the right places.

### FACT BOX

- Jigging is a high energy form of fishing and does not suit everyone.

- Cranking a heavy jig at full speed from 120 metres (360 ft) down will test the anglers endurance and fitness.

- It is easier in shallow water but it can still be physically demanding.

- "Young fella sport" is how one of our plain speaking customers rated it, and he's probably right.

- However, when the fish respond to the jigs it is possible to get repeated hook-ups and good catches.

- It is a fun and productive way to fish and it can help save on gym fees.

Huge yellowfin tuna will often come up a berley trail behind a drifting boat.
PHOTO: DAVID ROCHE

# CHAPTER 12

# DRIFT FISHING

Drifting along in the ocean currents using a combination of baits and berley to attract the fish is a popular and highly productive fishing technique.

It is most productive on tuna, albacore and sharks but it also catches a wide range of other species including marlin and broadbill swordfish at night.

## WHERE

The obvious place to drift is where the fish are most likely to be found. In most areas this will be a known fishing area, along a reef line, continental shelf, around underwater mountains or where fish look likely.

Places with current lines, working flocks of birds, clear changes in water colour or temperature or closely associated with bait schools are all ideal areas to drift.

There are also technical considerations to make when drifting and how this works on the target fish.

In places where the boat is drifting over an ocean feature, the drift may be repeated to place the boat over and through the main strike zone on a regular basis.

Where sharks are the target or open water drifting is being planned, anglers may catch more fish doing a day long drift and letting the berley or chum attract the fish to the back of the boat.

This is one point where the knowledge, experience and judgement of the skipper really counts for something. Learning the signs, being observant and knowing how to work an area can have a big bearing on catches. So it pays to learn fast.

## BOAT SKILLS

When drifting, the boats direction of drift will be affected by both the wind and the current and the direction of the bow of the boat.

The process starts by knowing what the weather is predicted to do. If there is a nor'east wind forecast

The classic prize, a 70 kg yellowfin tuna taken on a live slimy mackerel fished down the berley slick.

A solid yellowfin taken on a pillie is fought to the boat.

and the current is running at 1 knot from the north to the south then the combination of current and wind will probably drift the boat along at 1.5 to 2 knots an hour.

Over a six or eight hour drift this may see the boat covering 10 or 12 nautical miles. In a strong wind or current it may be double this so some calculations need to be made about where to start the drift.

Similarly if the current is from the north and the breeze is from the south this will tend to 'hold' the boat in the current and the distance drifted may be considerably shortened. Any fish attracted under these conditions will have to swim up current to reach the boat, but they will do this.

The aim of calculating the drift is to ensure you are not left with a rough and difficult trip home at the end of the day. If the wind is forecast from the north and the current is running from north to south then the ideal place to start will be in the desired depth but about 10 nautical miles north of the port.

This point is trolled to as a rule, allowing the anglers to assess water and bait as they go.

When the drift starts the boat is set across the current side on and will have some wind driven forward movement depending which way the bow points. This can be important at times as one way takes you back to shore into shallower water and the other takes you further out.

A black marlin hooked on a bait fights fiercely to throw the hook.

Both directions can be useful depending on where the skipper wants the boat to go.

## BERLEY

Laying down a berley slick is one of the keys to successful drift fishing. The berley is the means of attracting the fish and sharks to the boat although quite a few fish find the bait irrespective of the berley.

Fish like yellowfin tuna and sharks, are keen followers of a berley trail. Sharks are mostly attracted by the smell of the mash or pulped fish coming from the berley bucket. This is usually striped tuna (skipjack) or other small, oily fish not wanted for any other purpose.

Frames and heads of game fish taken previously for consumption can also be used as can mullet or other cheap commercial fish.

The berley can be spiced with a little tuna oil to add smell and to provide a calm 'window' at the back of the boat to spot any fish which may be cruising in the slick.

Tournament shark fisherman may take the berley side of things to extremes often using 200 kilograms (400 lb) or more of berley in a day by dropping large amounts of cut fish and 'trawler trash' over the side as they drift along. It gets results, particularly on big tiger sharks.

Yellowfin tuna on the other hand show very little

**Offshore drift and berleying.**

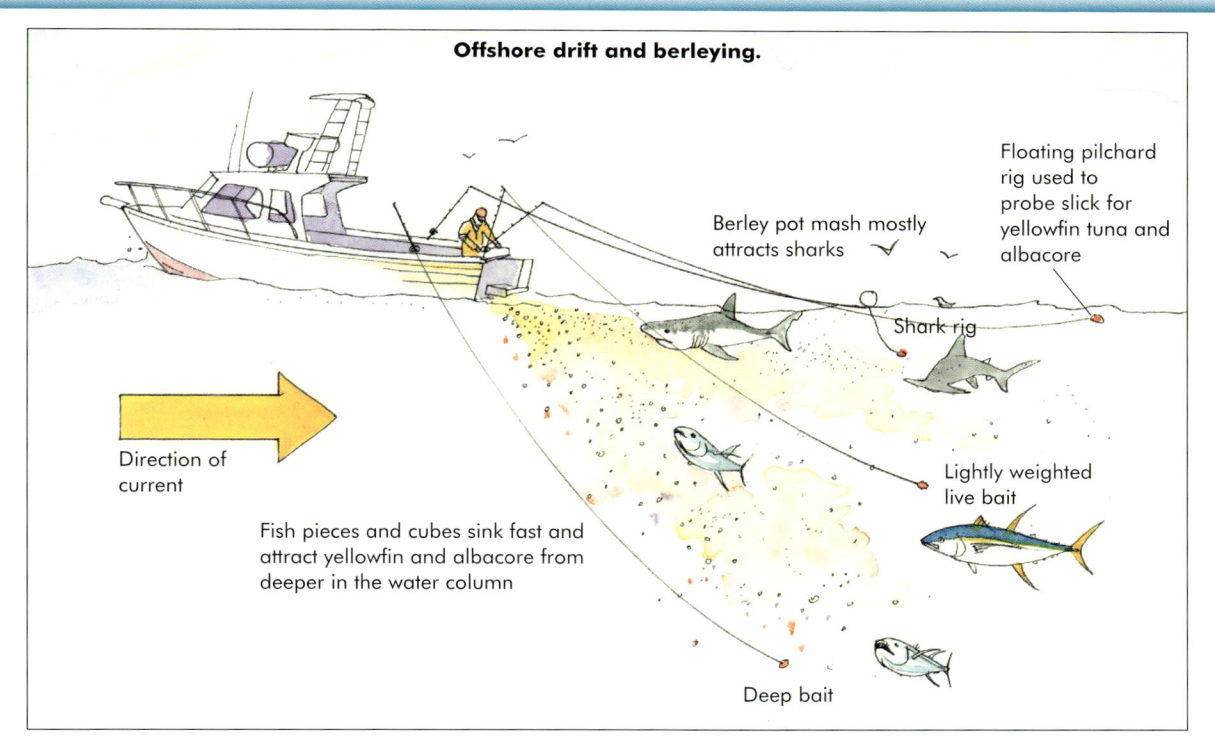

- Floating pilchard rig used to probe slick for yellowfin tuna and albacore
- Berley pot mash mostly attracts sharks
- Shark rig
- Direction of current
- Fish pieces and cubes sink fast and attract yellowfin and albacore from deeper in the water column
- Lightly weighted live bait
- Deep bait

interest in the berley pulp but are genuinely interested in small pieces of pilchards or other small bait fish dropped over the side. This is known as 'cubing'.

The term comes from years past when yellowfin and striped tuna were turned into 2 cm X 2 cm (1" X 1") cubes or chunks and dropped over the side for exactly the same purpose.

These days pilchards and any small bait fish are used. Their silvery gleam as they fall through the water layers draws yellowfin tuna, albacore and striped tuna (skipjack) like a magnet.

It also attracts its share of dolphin fish (mahi mahi) and marlin as well as sharks.

The pilchards and small fish are cut into three or four pieces and dropped over the side. As each series of pieces goes out of sight down the slick another two or three pieces are dropped over. This happens for the duration of the drift.

For most days, a minimum of 10 kilograms (20 lb) of pilchards is needed with 20 kilograms (40 lb) being plenty. Block pilchards can be used although 20 kg (40 lb) bulk blocks of second grade pilchards are available from fish co-operatives at very cheap prices.

Pilchards and pilchard pieces form the basis of cube trails and berley slicks for yellowfin.

## 92 BLUEWATER FISHING

## DRIFT RIGS FOR UPPER AND MID-LEVELS IN BERLEY TRAIL

Drift fishing rigs can be kept relatively simple although anglers need to set baits to cover a range of depths not just the surface.

The rigs set reflect the target fish and some anglers deliberately set no shark gear to avoid contact with them.

The rigs used depend on the target fish. Generally, a couple of live baits are set on the surface on 50 kg (100 lb) traces for yellowfin tuna. If marlin are a chance, the live bait furthest out is set on a 200 or

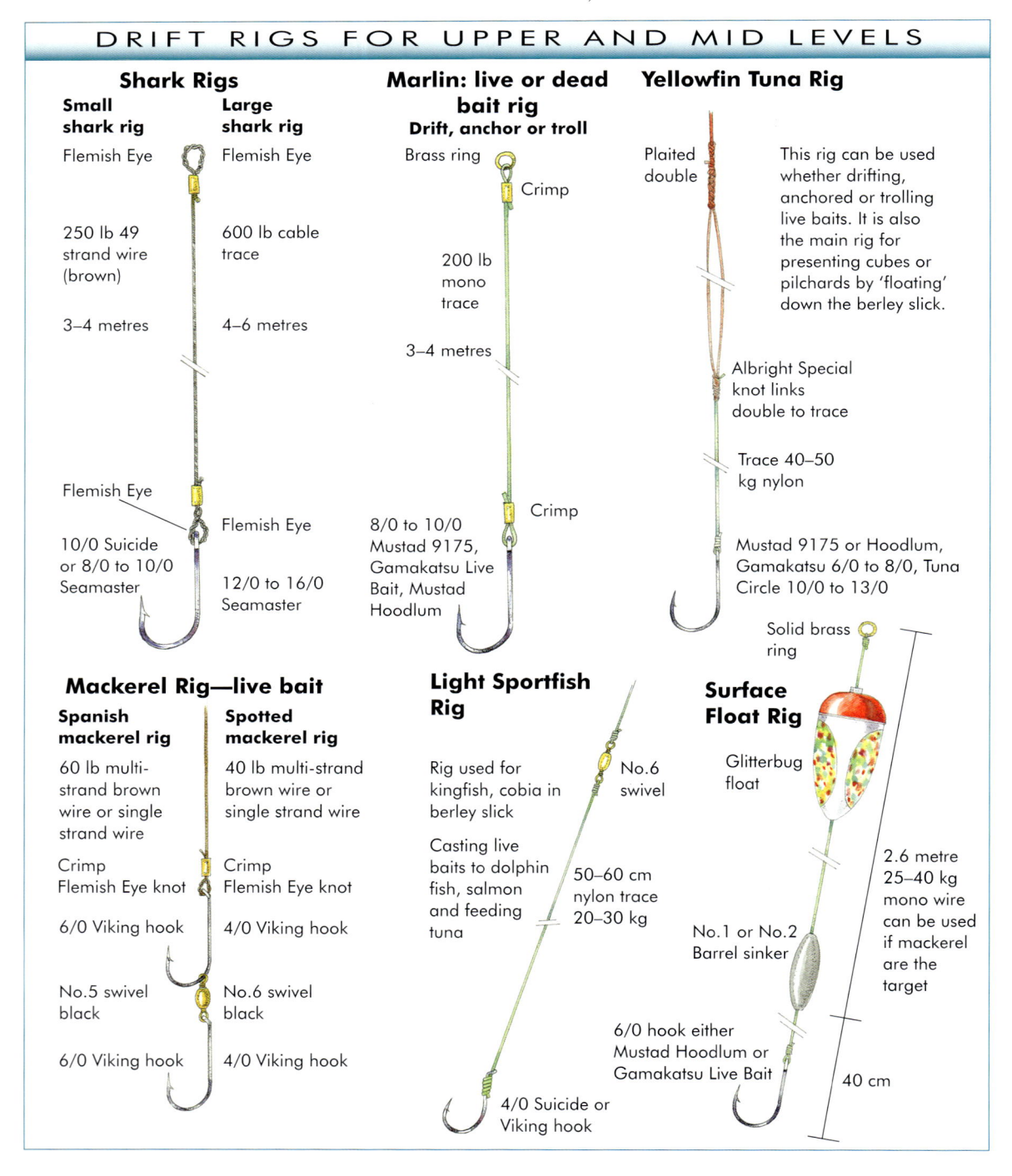

### DRIFT RIGS FOR UPPER AND MID LEVELS

#### Shark Rigs

**Small shark rig**
- Flemish Eye
- 250 lb 49 strand wire (brown)
- 3–4 metres
- Flemish Eye
- 10/0 Suicide or 8/0 to 10/0 Seamaster

**Large shark rig**
- Flemish Eye
- 600 lb cable trace
- 4–6 metres
- Flemish Eye
- 12/0 to 16/0 Seamaster

#### Marlin: live or dead bait rig
**Drift, anchor or troll**
- Brass ring
- Crimp
- 200 lb mono trace
- 3–4 metres
- Crimp
- 8/0 to 10/0 Mustad 9175, Gamakatsu Live Bait, Mustad Hoodlum

#### Yellowfin Tuna Rig
- Plaited double
- This rig can be used whether drifting, anchored or trolling live baits. It is also the main rig for presenting cubes or pilchards by 'floating' down the berley slick.
- Albright Special knot links double to trace
- Trace 40–50 kg nylon
- Mustad 9175 or Hoodlum, Gamakatsu 6/0 to 8/0, Tuna Circle 10/0 to 13/0

#### Mackerel Rig—live bait

**Spanish mackerel rig**
- 60 lb multi-strand brown wire or single strand wire
- Crimp Flemish Eye knot
- 6/0 Viking hook
- No.5 swivel black
- 6/0 Viking hook

**Spotted mackerel rig**
- 40 lb multi-strand brown wire or single strand wire
- Crimp Flemish Eye knot
- 4/0 Viking hook
- No.6 swivel black
- 4/0 Viking hook

#### Light Sportfish Rig
- Rig used for kingfish, cobia in berley slick
- Casting live baits to dolphin fish, salmon and feeding tuna
- No.6 swivel
- 50–60 cm nylon trace 20–30 kg
- 4/0 Suicide or Viking hook

#### Surface Float Rig
- Solid brass ring
- Glitterbug float
- 2.6 metre 25–40 kg mono wire can be used if mackerel are the target
- No.1 or No.2 Barrel sinker
- 6/0 hook either Mustad Hoodlum or Gamakatsu Live Bait
- 40 cm

300 lb trace. Marlin often wear through the more standard 50 kg (100 lb) nylon yellowfin tuna traces in fairly quick time, but it depends on where the hook ends up.

The 50 kg (100 lb) traces are attached to the main line using an Albright Special knot while the heavy traces are attached by snap swivels.

One or two weighted baits are also paid out. These can be live or dead baits or pilchards.

There are several methods of setting deep baits. Our favourite is to leave a long tag end when the 50 kg (100 lb) trace is joined to the main line. A Snapper or Bomb type sinker of any weight can then be attached.

Sinker weights relate to the depth you want to set the bait and the prevailing conditions. Usually sinkers of 200 to 450 grams (6oz to 1 lb) are used, but lighter sinkers can be chosen for baits set down 30 metres (90 ft) or so. The trace is 6 metres (18 ft) long.

These rigs can be effectively fished at 110 metres (330 ft) but are mostly set at 40 to 60 metres (120 to 180 ft), it depends on how much weight is added and the speed of the drift.

When a fish is hooked and played to the boat the lead is nipped off when the trace comes up and the trace is then wound onto the reel and the fish gaffed or tagged.

It is also easy to set the deep baits using downriggers. Pay out the rig and about 30 to 40 metres (90 to 120 ft) of line and attach it to the downrigger clip or use a light elastic band.

Lower the downrigger to the desired depth and set the rod.

If sharks are the target, set the baits in closer than the yellowfin tuna and marlin rigs, this often allows for a good look at the shark before it takes a bait and may permit the selective baiting of the shark with the most appropriate class of tackle. Shark baits are usually small whole tuna or large strip baits.

Finally, an outfit for floating a cube or pilchard unweighted down the slick is set up at the back of the boat. This outfit has a 50 kg (100 lb) trace joined to the double with an Albright Special and a 6/0 or 7/0 hook or 13/0 Tuna Circle.

The aim of this rig is to drift a pilchard, pilchard piece or tuna strip down the slick at exactly the same rate of drift as the berley. The pilchard or strip bait rig is usually paid out 40 to 50 metres (120 to 150 ft) and left for a couple of minutes. It is then retrieved, often by hand, coiling it neatly on the floor of the boat or wound back onto the reel.

The process is repeated every five minutes or so until a fish hooks up. The reels are always set with enough drag to stop any over run but running free enough to be able to strip line by hand as needed. Many big yellowfin tuna fall to this rig.

With the baits set and a berley trail growing in length there is a waiting game to be played. Sometimes the fish turn up fast, sometimes it takes a few hours, sometimes nothing happens. Drifting can be like that, so can any type of game fishing.

## INSHORE DRIFTING

Drifting can be an effective method of catching inshore game fish like yellowtail kingfish, cobia, mackerel, sharks and other sportfish.

The important points in drifting are to learn the areas where the target fish hold, position the boat to drift over the most productive area and use rigs that are effective on the fish being chased.

In some places, drifting is the most effective fishing method available.

Sometimes it can be the only method, particularly if a stiff current is running and anchoring is out of the question.

Tiger sharks are highly attracted to a fishy berley trail.

**Reef profile for inshore sportfish.**

Direction of current

## HITTING THE SPOT

Knowing where the fish are schooling or feeding is an essential part of this type of fishing.

In most areas, the fish are spread over the reefs or rocky ledges and the drifting boat works through these, presenting baits to the fish as it drifts along.

In specific cases fish are targeted on pinnacles, ledges and drop offs. The boat is positioned over these and the baits are dropped into whatever is showing on the echo sounder.

If the fish are there the results usually come fast and the rods curve over as the live baits are taken.

The boat moves from spot to spot looking for target fish and dropping live baits or squid on them.

This technique is deadly on yellowtail kingfish, samson fish and amberjack but needs plenty of live baits and a good selection of reefs in the GPS.

Spanish and spotted mackerel are often well spread over reef country and a combination of drifted pilchards and live baits can be highly effective.

Drifting can be short to target specific reefs, drop offs, current lines or longer where there is an extensive fishing area with fish spread around.

Drifting for table fish can also be done at the same time and in the same areas where the sportfish are found.

## DRIFT RIGS FOR DEEPER WATER

Drift rigs for bottom dwelling game fish are usually heavily weighted and are designed to get to the bottom quickly and stay straight up and down during the drift.

The usual technique is to hook the live bait through the top of the nose and out under the chin (to minimise

*The tag pole is readied for a big shark hooked off Port Stephens.*

## DRIFT RIGS FOR UPPER AND MID LEVELS

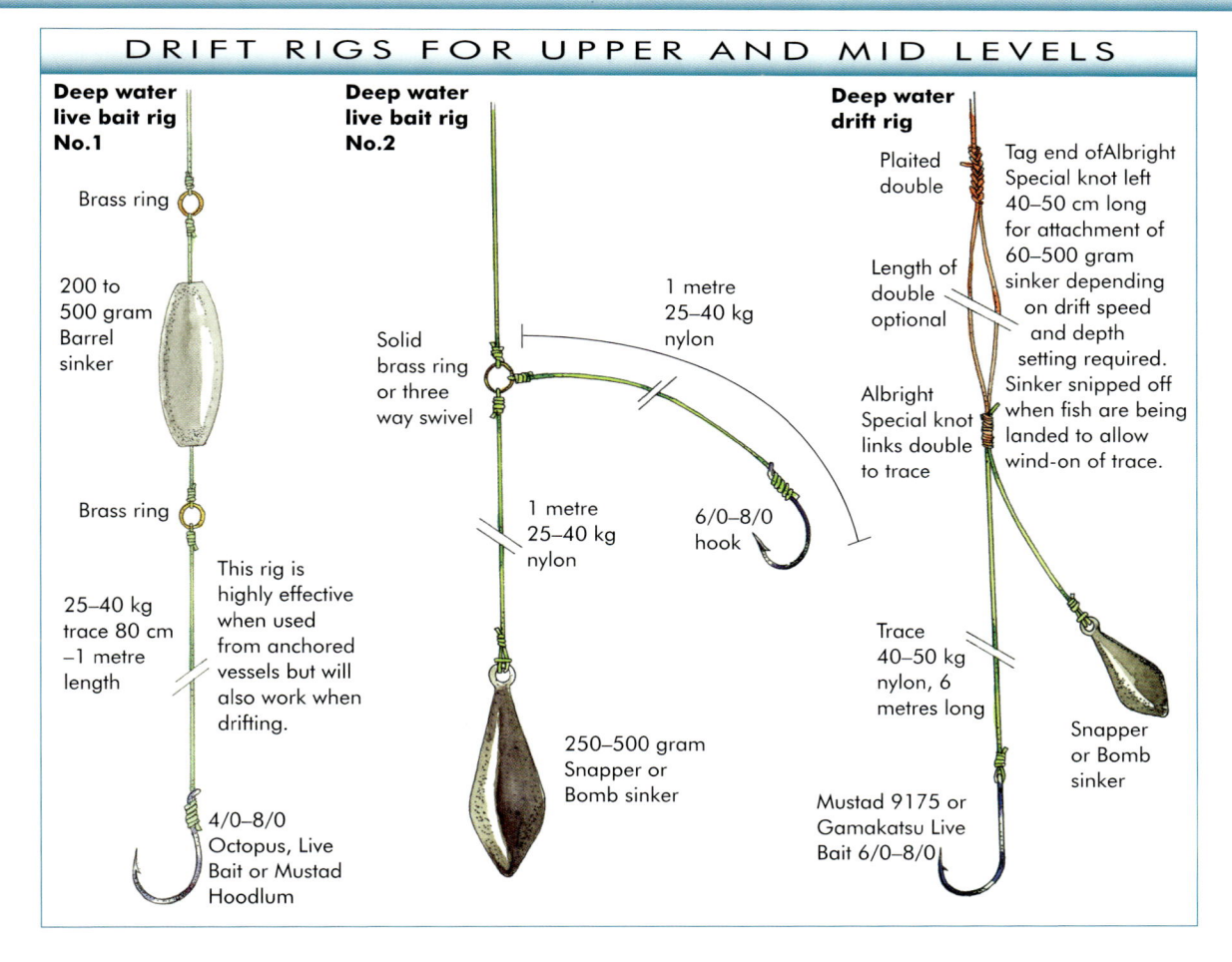

**Deep water live bait rig No.1**
- Brass ring
- 200 to 500 gram Barrel sinker
- Brass ring
- 25–40 kg trace 80 cm –1 metre length
- 4/0–8/0 Octopus, Live Bait or Mustad Hoodlum

**Deep water live bait rig No.2**
- Solid brass ring or three way swivel
- 1 metre 25–40 kg nylon
- 1 metre 25–40 kg nylon
- 6/0–8/0 hook
- 250–500 gram Snapper or Bomb sinker

This rig is highly effective when used from anchored vessels but will also work when drifting.

**Deep water drift rig**
- Plaited double
- Length of double optional
- Albright Special knot links double to trace
- Tag end of Albright Special knot left 40–50 cm long for attachment of 60–500 gram sinker depending on drift speed and depth setting required. Sinker snipped off when fish are being landed to allow wind-on of trace.
- Trace 40–50 kg nylon, 6 metres long
- Snapper or Bomb sinker
- Mustad 9175 or Gamakatsu Live Bait 6/0–8/0

---

spin) and drop the rig to the bottom. The lead is then lifted one or two rod lifts clear of the bottom and the rod held awaiting the strike or set in a rod holder.

The baits distance off the bottom can be checked every couple of minutes by letting the sinker hit the bottom and then lifting the rig clear by one or two rod lifts.

Mackerel rigs are always made up on wire and drifted live baits are worked on stinger type rigs if the drift is fast or on a standard live bait rig if the drift is slow. Pilchards are usually presented on three hook gangs with a wire trace, or with a single hook through the nose.

## STRIKE

When deep water drifted live baits are taken the angler should allow the fish to put a solid bend in the rod before leaning back to sink the hook. Do not strike as soon as a take is felt.

If the rod is in a rod holder allow the fish to pull the rod right over and for line to move off the spool before picking up the rod. The fish will have hooked itself and need not be struck.

Mackerel baits are drifted on the surface and in mid water with the reels in gear and the drags set at strike level. When a bait is taken the drag sets the hook and the fish is on.

*Cobia regularly appear in berley trails and around inshore reefs.*

Sunset, at anchor and expectations are high.
PHOTO: DAVID ROCHE

# CHAPTER 13

# FISHING AT ANCHOR

Fishing at anchor is used to catch reef dwelling sportfish and game fish that feed around reefs and similar structures.

It is used extensively wherever reef areas provide a focus for fishing activity.

Locating the boat securely over the main fish holding area maximises captures and provides a platform for a range of fishing techniques to be applied.

In general terms anchoring most boats is feasible in water depths out to about 120 to 150 metres (360 to 450 ft). As the depths increase anchoring over a dedicated spot becomes harder and harder.

## EQUIPMENT

Anchoring is a fairly exact science because it is vital that the boat ends up somewhere not just anywhere. To do this properly the ground tackle of anchors, chains and rope needs to be right.

Most small craft use reef picks with prongs that can be straightened by the boat driving ahead to get them off. Larger craft use either large reef anchors or arrow head anchors (Maloolabah Pick) that are 'tripped' so they can be released from the bottom, or CQR anchors dropped in sand or mud and then the boat is positioned over the reef with the anchor rope.

The secret of good reef anchors is to keep the prongs short like a grappling hook, this provides the best grip on the reef and will not straighten easily if the wind blows hard. Long pronged picks have no gripping strength as the leverage needed to straighten them is minimal.

Trim the prongs short with a hacksaw and then bend them into place. Bending into a round shape is important. Use the ball of your foot for small craft anchors and 100 mm (4 ins) pipe to shape larger anchors.

The chain used is just as important as the anchor.

Yellowtail kingfish are a regular target for reef fishing anglers.

**Fishing at anchor.**

Direction of current

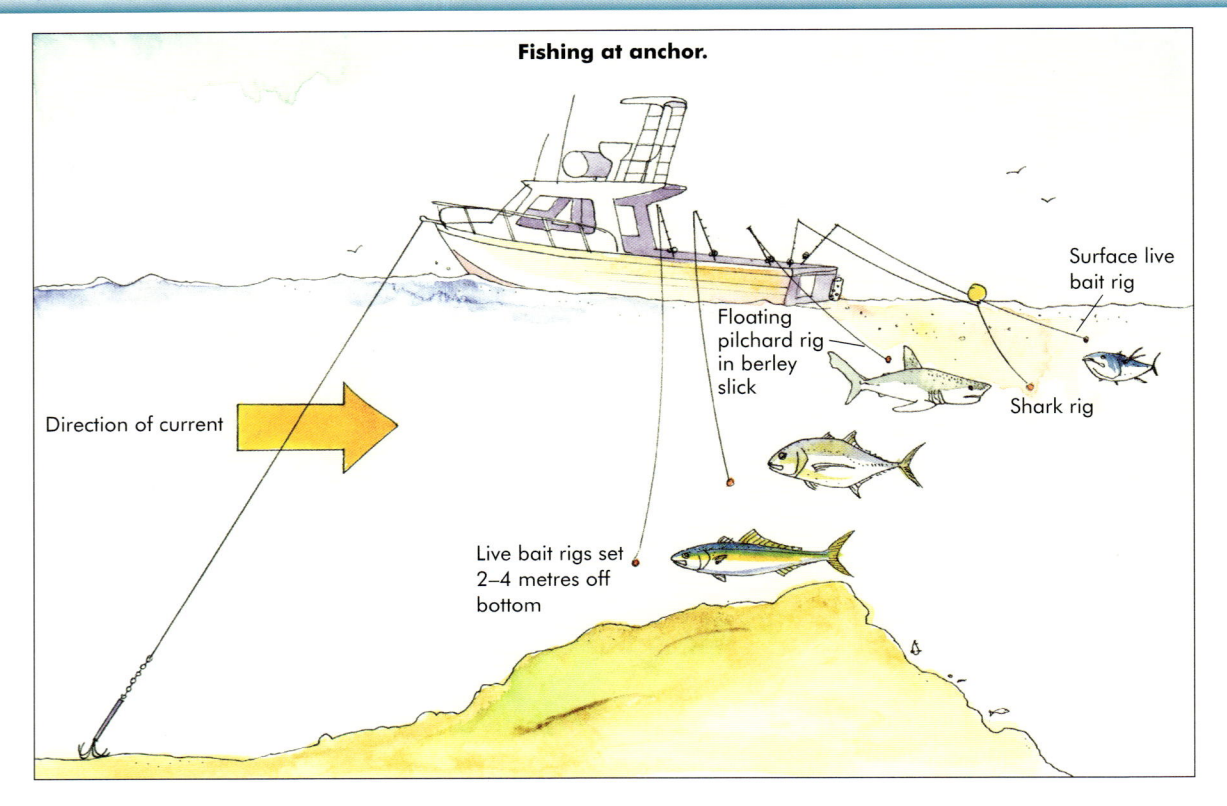

Floating pilchard rig in berley slick

Surface live bait rig

Shark rig

Live bait rigs set 2–4 metres off bottom

Chain stops the anchor rope wearing on the bottom but far more importantly it both sets the anchor in the bottom and acts as a shock absorber for the boat as it rises and falls in the swell.

Anchor chains should be 4 to 6 metres (12 to 18 ft) long in most boats with a chain gauge of 6 to 10 mm (2.5 to 4 ins) depending on the size of the boat. A heavy anchor chain will ensure a smooth ride for the boat on the anchor and a better grip on the bottom.

A shark gaffed and tail roped on a moored boat off Sydney. Note the dan buoy on the bow ready to drop if necessary.

## SETTING THE ANCHOR

The most important part of reef fishing is to be anchored where the fish are. This may seem obvious, but too many anglers are just content to be on the reef and don't worry about the finer points of the craft.

It is the anglers who do take the trouble to get things right who catch the most fish.

The first job then is to use the sounder to establish either where the fish are or often more importantly that part of the reef where the fish are most likely to be.

For fish like yellowtail kingfish, samson fish, amberjack, mackerel and trevally this usually means being moored over the high ground on top of the reef.

Anglers looking for table fish may also choose this spot although many look for the reef edge where it drops onto the sand, gravel or coral rubble for their table fish.

Yellowfin tuna can be fished for at anchor and most boats chasing them fish the higher points of the reef. Where a drop-off or edge is evident it may be wise to anchor along this and then let the tuna run out into deeper water

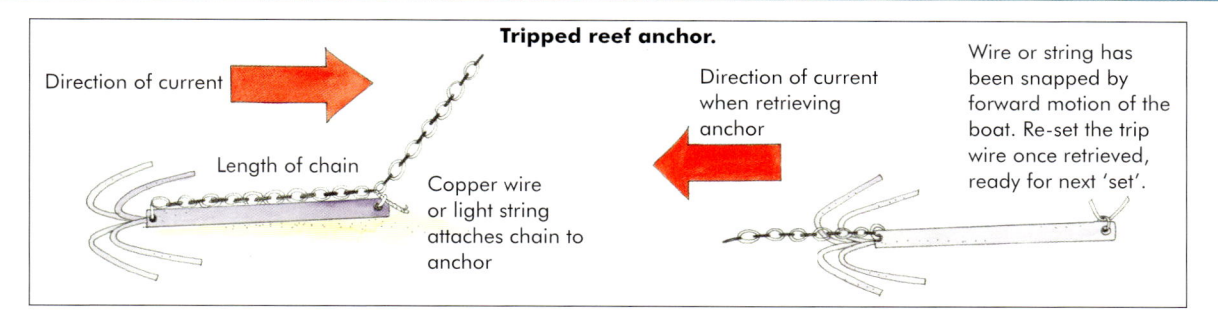

# Fishing at Anchor

**Tripped reef anchor.**

Direction of current

Length of chain

Copper wire or light string attaches chain to anchor

Direction of current when retrieving anchor

Wire or string has been snapped by forward motion of the boat. Re-set the trip wire once retrieved, ready for next 'set'.

Once the preferred anchoring location is established, the other factors like wind and current are assessed as these will determine where the boat finishes and which way it will sit on the anchor rope.

Generally, current direction and speed will have the prevailing effect on where the boat sits but the wind, if any, or expected to pick up from a known direction, can have considerable influence if current strengths are low.

Always check the way any other boats in the area are sitting on their anchors as this is the way your boat will also sit.

Drive the boat forward of the selected anchoring spot, into the wind and current, usually allowing about 50 metres (150 ft) for the anchor to drop and bite into the bottom. In deeper water or in strong current this may need to be extended to 80 or 100 metres (240 to 300 ft).

Once the anchor locks into the bottom the boat is usually close to the preferred spot and perhaps 10 or 20 metres (30 or 60 ft) of rope may need to be payed out to position the vessel exactly.

Secure the rope and set the dan buoy if fishing for game fish and then set the baits.

**Setting and retrieving a reef anchor.**

Dan Buoy

Mooring line

Rubber plumbers ring

Direction of current

Chain and reef pick

Direction of current

For safety reasons all anchors at sea are pulled by driving forward into the current, pulling the anchor from the bottom. The boat continues to move forward with increased speed once anchor is free. The dan bouy can be used to assist with the retrieveal of the anchor and chain.

One way stainless steel snap clip

Water pressure as boat travels forward forces dan buoy along anchor rope until it hits chain. The one way clip prevents clip sliding back up rope. Anchor rope is retrieved as vessel drifts back to dan buoy.

## DAN BUOY

The dan buoy is a large float that has two uses. It is used to easily retrieve the anchor by simply driving the boat ahead and letting water pressure on the buoy and force it and its one way clip along the rope. The large stainless one way clip used to attach it to the rope slides along the rope and then onto the chain, holding the anchor and chain on the surface as the boat drifts back to it and the rope is retrieved.

# 100 BLUEWATER FISHING

*Rigs everywhere and a good Spanish mackerel coming to the boat. Sorting out the fish from the rest of the gear can sometimes be an issue.*

from the bow as this will also cushion the ride at anchor and all they need to do is start the engine and drop the rope once a fish hooks up.

## FISHING SET UP

Fishing at anchor is often done with just one species in mind, by selectively choosing a reef or structure where those fish live. This particularly applies to mackerel, yellowfin tuna, yellowtail kingfish and amberjack but it depends on the location.

More generally, it is possible to set for both the target species plus any other fish that are known to be in the area.

If the fishing is confined to one species or one style then the rigs are set, berley is started and all the anglers need to do is wait for a hook up. To pass the time, many anglers then fish for table fish or toss lures or jigs.

When fishing selectively, always ensure baits are set to cover all the possibilities. A couple of baits on the bottom, one in mid water and one or two on the surface.

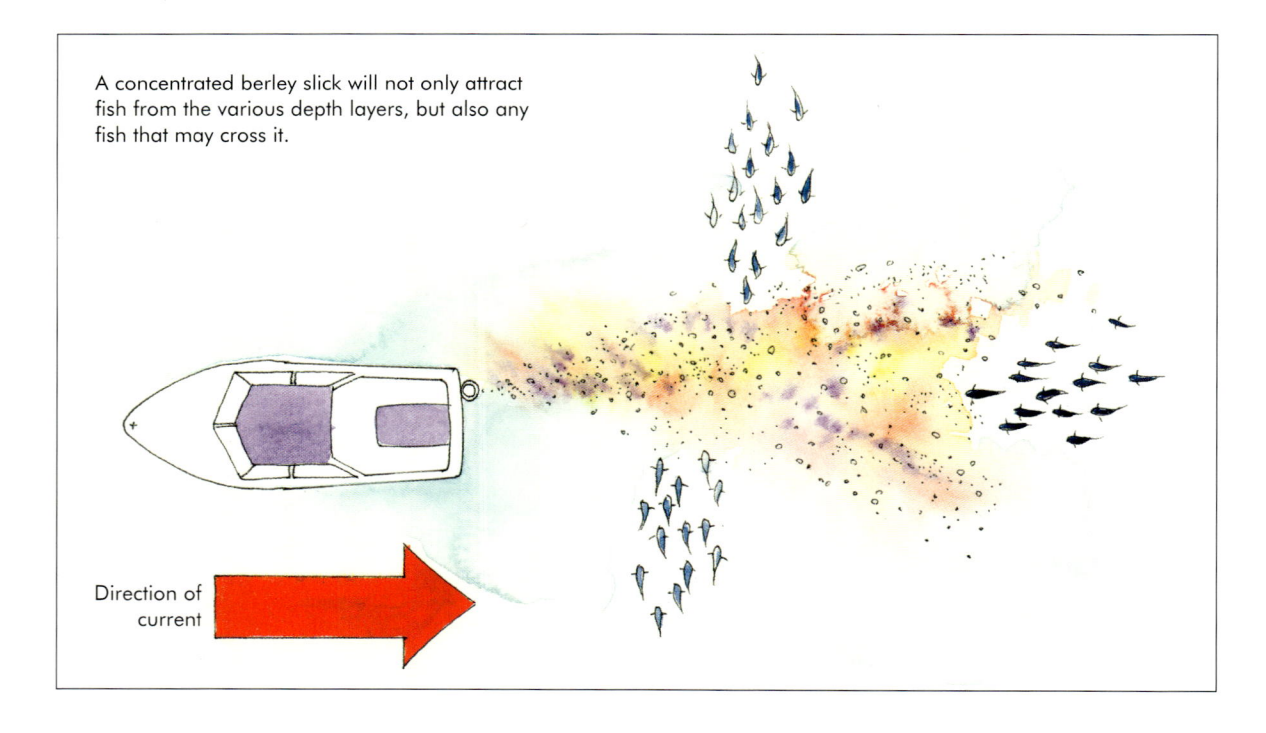

The second use is once the boat is moored a blind loop is put in the rope and the snap clip attaches the buoy to the anchor rope so it can be dropped if a hard running fish hooks up. The spare coils of rope are tied so they can be dropped over the side together with the buoy to chase the fish.

Many boats set the buoy about 10 metres (30 ft)

*A concentrated berley slick will not only attract fish from the various depth layers, but also any fish that may cross it.*

Direction of current

On mackerel, it is usual to concentrate on surface and mid water baits although a bait set 2 to 4 metres (6 to 12 ft) off the bottom can often turn a surprising number of mackerel.

Where a range of fish are possible the key is to cover the options. A couple of surface baits rigged with the trace linked by an Albright Special knot and 50 to 60 kg (100 to 120 lb) leader will take yellowfin tuna and give a chance should a marlin hook up. Yellowtail kingfish will also be likely to take this bait. One of the yellowfin tuna rigs can be lightly weighted and set under a float to work a little deeper than the other. An unweighted pilchard or cube can be floated back down the berley if yellowfin tuna are in the area.

A dead bonito, frigate mackerel or large live bait can be set on 250 lb 49 strand wire and a 10/0 hook for sharks and buoyed with a float well back. Marlin also have a habit of picking this bait up as well.

Yellowtail kingfish rigs are then set about 2 metres (6 ft) off the bottom and the boat is then ready for whatever comes up the berley trail or takes a bait. If yellowtail kingfish are the primary target, a weighted bait set half way down or a little deeper can often turn a few extra fish.

Berley is usually both mash from the berley pot and cubes of cut pilchards or small bait fish. If there is current to hold the rigs in place it is also feasible to use downriggers to set the mid water baits.

Tropical anglers can do similar things for their reef fish. With mackerel rigs on top and then a range of gear for deeper feeding fish and reef fish. The catch and strike rate is optimised by covering the water column and the fish likely to be feeding in the area.

The ideal situation for a moored boat. The fish are on and the buoy is already set out the front if they need to chase the fish.

Yellowtail kingfish are a regular target for reef fishing anglers.

Spotted mackerel are a popular fish for vessels moored over reefs in warmer waters.

## CATCHING FISH

When setting the rigs at anchor always note the amount of current running as this will effect the live baits and govern the amount of lead needed to hold the baits in position. In heavy current, always hook the live baits through the nose from side to side. This holds them head first into the current allowing them to breath and swim.

In low current they can be either nose hooked or hooked through the shoulder area. Baits hooked near the tail region will die quickly as they end up tail-on to the current and cannot breathe properly.

Yellowfin tuna and yellowtail kingfish rigs are set with the drag at strike level while the shark rig is set with just enough drag to prevent an overrun.

Mackerel rigs are similarly set under floats or balloons, with the drags firmly set.

Yellowtail kingfish, samson fish, amberjack, big trevally, cobia and similar bottom fish mostly fight up and down or around the boat and don't take enough line to worry about leaving the anchor.

Big tuna, marlin and sharks are almost always better fought from a moving vessel free of an anchor rope. In general terms, any fish that takes more than half a spool of line forces the dan buoy to be dropped and the fish chased. If the fish is going to be chased, make the decision fast and get going.

In popular spots with plenty of other boats around it is often wise to drop the dan buoy and get clear of the mob as quickly as possible rather than have a big fish run amok near other vessels's anchor ropes.

Once the fish has been fought and landed the boat returns to the dan buoy, ties up, re-sets the gear and waits for the next strike.

*Mulloway are one of the great prizes when fishing from moored vessels.*

---

### FACT BOX
# COBIA

Cobia are one of the strangest looking of all the game fish. Their body shape and colour looks almost exactly like a shark, although they lack teeth and have a small dorsal fin.

Their shark like appearance has led many anglers to break them off at first sight, before realising exactly what they were fighting.

They are mostly encountered around inshore reefs and are relatively common in warmer temperate and tropical waters.

Cobia often take baits and lures intended for mackerel or surprise reef fishermen by grabbing a cut bait on the bottom. They also appear regularly in the berley slick and will readily take a pilchard or other bait fish. Again, the fish in the berley are often called as sharks and ignored until someone wakes up to what they really are.

Cobia will take the full range of baits and lures but are usually more attracted to live baits, rigged gars and minnow type lures.

They can fight dirty in rough reef country but they are nowhere near as contrary as big yellowtail kingfish in the same area. Their big tail and muscular body ensures a long fight with the larger fish.

At the end, they can be easily tagged and released and have a high survival rate or gaffed as a first rate table fish.

104 BLUEWATER FISHING

Pearl perch provide sweet eating fillets of the highest quality.

# CHAPTER 14

# BOTTOM AND REEF FISHING

There are two sides to bottom and reef fishing. One is chasing the genuine reef dwelling brawlers like yellowtail kingfish, amberjack, great trevally, samson fish, dog tooth tuna and cobia. The other is more simply related to the catching of a feed of snapper, cod, grouper, coral trout, emperor or whatever tasty table fish happen to live there.

The two types of fishing are very similar only the emphasis on different targets change.

## WHERE

The most important part of reef fishing is knowing where the reefs are in a fishing zone and knowing which fish species can be found where. Some of this information is sometimes available from maps and publications, some will be gleaned from local knowledge and some simply by using the echo sounder and finding likely looking pieces of geography.

*Premium snapper are the focus for many bottom fishing anglers.*

**Bottom fishing rig and bait options.**

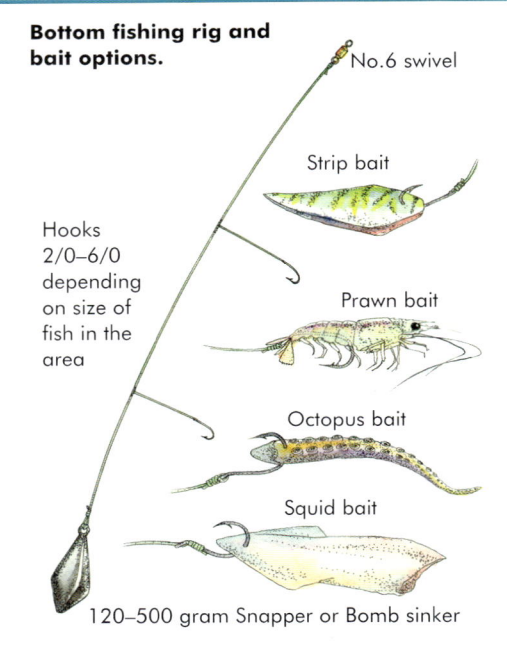

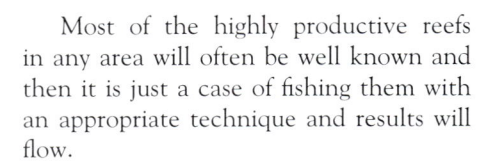

- No.6 swivel
- Strip bait
- Hooks 2/0–6/0 depending on size of fish in the area
- Prawn bait
- Octopus bait
- Squid bait
- 120–500 gram Snapper or Bomb sinker

Set gear to work surface, mid-water and bottom

Securely anchor vessel clear of wave break zone

Direction of current

Use berley trail to attract fish

**Working inshore headland, island or bommie.**

Most of the highly productive reefs in any area will often be well known and then it is just a case of fishing them with an appropriate technique and results will flow.

## DEPTH

Water depths being fished vary from place to place but there has been a general swing worldwide for anglers to fish deeper and deeper water as harder fished inshore reefs become less productive.

This trend has been facilitated by braided lines, improved fishing tackle and in really deep water, electric reels. While anglers have always wanted to work deeper they now have the technology to do so.

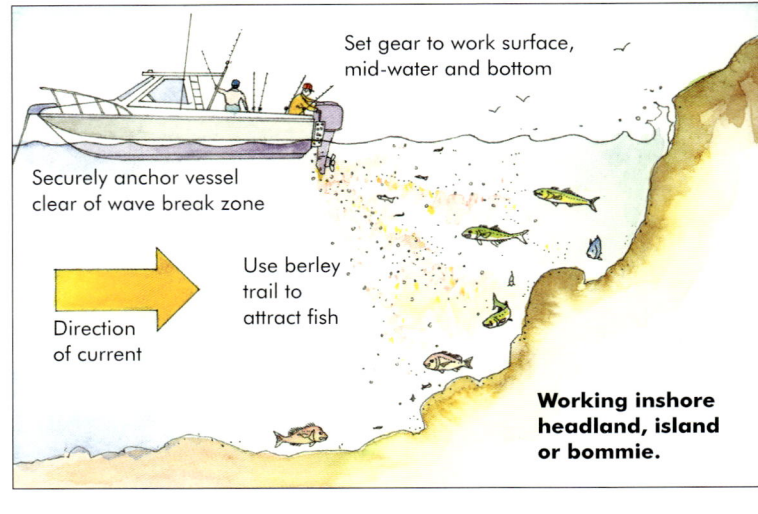

Bar cod are one of the great prizes for deepwater anglers.

## TACKLE

The tackle used for bottom fishing has evolved to meet the demands of tough fish being fought straight up and down. Reels need low gearing to provide more crank power. Rods have light tips for bite sensitivity but rapidly fall away into a firm middle section for lifting fish out of the depths.

Straight up and down fights transmit a lot of weight and stress onto the anglers back so quality rod buckets and lightweight harnesses can help during longer fights.

The genuine game fish of the deep reefs have more than just physical power, they have the added advantage of being able to reef the angler or cut off in coral or kelp.

The use of braided lines has helped a lot, with its limited stretch allowing more direct pressure on the fish.

The emphasis on using IGFA or sportfishing line classes has also gone out the window. The aim is to beat the fish. Anglers now have both overhead and threadline reels capable of working 50 lb or 80 lb

Tropical fish like these nannygai make great eating.

Coral trout are a major target species in tropical waters.

braid with 20 to 35 lb drag settings.

It's a rough, tough game but bigger and better reef brawlers are being caught because of the tackle available.

The gear and the techniques may appear brutal but the results are far better than being comprehensively trashed by fish after fish on light tackle.

## TABLE FISH

Catching table fish like snapper, cod, coral trout, grouper, flatfish, mulloway and other tasty reef dwellers is always an option for bluewater anglers.

Some boats do nothing else except chase these fish. Many anglers view reef fishing or bottom bouncing as their preferred style of fishing.

The uncomplicated rig is set on a heavy lead, lower the bait to the bottom and wait for a bite. It is basic fishing at it's best.

When the fish bites the rod is lifted to set the hook and then the angler winds it to the boat where it is netted or gaffed aboard.

The surprise packet of not knowing what fish is on the line and the genuine eating qualities of the premium table fish available in this type of fishing also adds to its attraction.

The low stress and low input side of the fishing also contributes to its popularity as a relaxing day on the water.

The key to catching good fish is to know the reefs and then work the edges or pinnacles where the good fish often hold. Many of the fish are easy to find on the echo sounder and the boat is then positioned to drift over or through that area.

Sometimes it is best to moor the boat over the reef or structure and use berley to attract the fish around the boat.

In this style of fishing both weighted bottom baits and lightly weighted 'floating' baits are used. The lightly weighted baits are worked down the berley trail to catch fish feeding on the stream of tit bits available.

In coral areas the same principles apply. There are often good fish on the deeper reefs and many anglers also work the coral drop-offs and passages between the coral reefs.

No matter where the fishing is done, the keys are to keep the rigs neat and simple and to use the geography to find the fish. Good bait, sharp hooks and appropriate tackle will make sure there is something good to eat on most days.

As with all table fish, make sure there is ice on board to care for the catch. Nothing improves the flavour of fish like plenty of ice.

Enjoy the catching and eating, it is one of the real treats being an angler can bring to both family and friends.

## RIGS

Rigs for bottom fishing are fairly basic and change very little around the world. Usually a Snapper or Bomb type sinker on the bottom and a couple of hooks on droppers is all that is needed to get started. The same rig with a heavier sinker is used for drift fishing. A trace of heavier line than the main line is used just in case a big fish takes the bottom bait.

The rigs for more specialised fishing are really only variations on other well known rigs. For instance, snapper floaters are a variation of an estuary drift rig with a sinker running down to a swivel and then 40 to 50 cm (16 to 20 ins) of 15 kg (30 lb) trace to a 2/0 or 4/0 hook.

The rig as the name suggests will catch snapper and other fish out of the berley trail. The sinker is usually a No. 2 or No. 3 Ball, just enough to carry the bait down towards the bottom. The sinker is also varied to suit the depth being fished and the speed of the current.

Mulloway are caught fishing on the reef edges and gutters. Similarly many of the prized coral species are caught on the deeper edges of the reefs and around large submerged reefs in deep water that provide habitat for the big fish.

The bottom rig does not need to change for coral fish, only the hooks are larger, with 4/0 to 6/0 being popular.

Many anglers working the coral reefs also fish lightly weighted pilchards particularly for coral trout. The technique is not much different to snapper fishing only the lines used are heavier and the hooks a little bigger.

## EXPERIENCE COUNTS

While bottom fishing can be reduced to fairly basic elements and some fish will still be caught, premium results only come from learning about the fish and where they live.

It is all part of the fun of bluewater angling and sometimes the sport and game fish won't bite so bottom fishing is the only option. At other times, catching a feed of premium table fish is part of the day and good eating fish are always welcome.

Light game tackle is ideal for many game fish and only requires the addition of a rod bucket.
PHOTO: BILL CLASSON

## CHAPTER 15

# HOOKING AND FIGHTING FISH

There are many opinions on how to hook and fight fish even amongst experienced charter boat skippers.

The truth is that there are a few techniques which do work and then anglers put their own variations on the theme. Each different type of fish needs some consideration to achieve the best possible hook up.

Applying a little thought to the process definitely improves the percentages, but nothing helps as much as regular fishing.

Running through a few scenarios with the main bluewater species and techniques is probably the best way to cover the various options.

## TROLLING LURES

Most anglers set their trolling reels in gear with a firm strike drag and let the fish run into razor sharp hooks. This produces an instant hook up and is the most reliable method on almost all fish.

Some lure trolling marlin anglers set their reels with light drags, for example, 1 or 2 kg (2 to 4 lb) of pressure and let the fish turn and run before pushing the lever to strike drag.

This technique needs trained crew and from our experience does not produce any more or less hook ups than conventional methods.

## LIVE BAIT TROLLING

For all fish, except mackerel, trolled live baits are set with just enough drag to prevent an over run. When a fish takes a bait it is allowed to run and swallow the bait.

*Threadline tackle needs firm control and the ability to keep the fish moving through the water towards the boat.*

The basic rule is the bigger the bait the more time given although most marlin get the baits down quite quickly.

On smaller baits like frigate mackerel and slimy mackerel 10 to 15 seconds is usually enough time.

*Good team work between the angler, skipper and crew draws this marlin closer to the tag pole.*

Experience plays a part here too. If a fish screams off and keeps going, or in the case of a marlin, starts jumping, plainly it has already felt the sting of the hook and the answer is to push the lever to strike and get some bend in the rod.

Mostly the bait will be taken in a quick surge and there is often a very faint pause as the bait is swallowed (remember the boat is still going forward so line will be lost continuously), and then the fish moves off again.

On mackerel the baits are set so that there is a hook in the strike zone and the reels are set with a firm drag to push the hooks home on the strike.

## YELLOWFIN TUNA

When fishing live baits for tuna other than striped tuna (skipjack) or frigate mackerel all rods are set in the strike position. This applies to cube, strip and pilchard baits as well.

Let the fish run into the hook, they engulf the baits anyway and a certain hook up will follow. Leave the rod in the rod holder and let the fish hook itself particularly when using Tuna Circle hooks.

## SHARKS

Most shark baits are set on wire and reels are set with just enough drag to prevent an over-run. Sharks often fool around with the baits and need time to get them down.

Once the shark has moved off with the bait the lever goes to strike and the hook is driven home as the weight comes onto the rod.

Sharks regularly grab baits set on mono for other game fish and when this is seen to happen just slide the drag lever to strike and let the shark run into the hook.

Often the hook will lodge in the corner of the mouth and the shark can be fought to a tag or gaff.

## OTHER GAME FISH

Most other game fish are best treated like yellowfin tuna. Set the reel with the drag at strike and let them run into the hook, they will hook themselves.

Holding the rod and striking at the fish misses more fish than it hooks. With the rod securely set in a rod holder let the fish do all the work.

Wind on leaders allow the fish to be fought right to the gaff or tag pole which can reduce some of the drama beside the boat.

Classic pose, a millpond calm day, a big fish and the angler giving it everything.

## STRIKE

Setting the hook when needed is done by sliding the lever to strike and winding until the weight of the fish comes onto the rod. Only when there is weight against the rod is the rod lifted firmly to drive home the hook.

There is no point striking at fish which have taken a trolled lure on a rod with the drag set at strike. The fish is already hooked and no amount of striking will alter that fact.

Striking in this situation can lead to break offs as the line is already stretched so any extra tension may force the line to part.

There is no need to try and rip the fish's teeth out either. Some anglers hit the fish with a lift and strike that almost throws them backwards. All this does is break lines. Sharp hooks bite in with a lift of the rod on a firm drag setting.

## SETTING THE DRAG

The aim of setting a drag is to ensure that the fish cannot break the line when it hooks up and it will then smoothly pay out line under controlled pressure whenever the fish runs.

Seems simple doesn't it. If it is so simple why do so many anglers break off?

The answer is that their drags are set too tight. Oceanic fish do not break you off, you break them off. Reef and coral dwellers can and do break anglers off, but that's another story later in this chapter.

Most game fishing reels with lever drags can be pre-set with a strike drag then more pressure is available by deliberately pushing the lever through the pre-set strike to a point where break off is very close. These settings are achieved either by checking the drag tension against a set of scales and calibrating the drag to match or in the hands of experienced anglers simply by feel.

The rule of thumb is that strike drag should never be more than one third of the breaking strain of the line. For example, the spool should start paying line when 5 kilograms (10 lb) of drag is showing on the scales when using 15 kg (30 lb) line or 8 kg (16 lb) on 24 kg (50 lb) line. This is also a good place to leave the drag setting when fighting most fish. Going for more drag only invites a break off.

The one third strike drag also presumes near new line and everything else in the system to be perfect.

Our experience suggests that most outfits stay connected best when set at a bit less than one third, say 4 kg (8 lb) of drag on 15 kg (30 lb) and 6½ kg (13 lb) on 24 kg (50 lb). If more power is needed once the fight settles down then it can be accessed by sliding the drag lever forward.

There is no magic exactly right number, so long as the drag used makes the tackle perform well and beats the fish, then everything is fine.

Many fishing writers, and therefore many anglers, stress the need to fish the tackle at its maximum performance level. This only loses fish.

It is a little like driving a racing car at its absolute maximum revs and speed and then being surprised when the engine blows or the car runs off the road.

Far more fish are landed by anglers who fish their gear at conservative but realistic settings than those who want everything running on the red line.

As a guide, if the line is crackling off the reel applying any more drag will break the line and a slight reduction in drag would probably be a good idea.

Using star drag reels does not offer the performance of a known pre-set and while a drag can be set most anglers working star drag reels soon learn to get the drag performance close to right just by pulling line off the reel by hand.

While oceanic fish should never break off because of too much drag, catching tough fish around the reefs can be an entirely different ball game.

Yellowtail kingfish, samson fish, amberjack, cobia (to a lesser extent), coral trout and big trevally can all deliberately wipe out anglers by diving into a reef, cave, kelp, coral or whatever they do to break the line.

When hooked up to a big fish that can and will reef the angler it is important to maintain as much pressure as possible without breaking off in order to turn the fish and start fighting it to the surface.

While it is possible for the fish to wipe out the angler, the angler should never put on so much pressure that they break off before the fish does the job in the reef.

Use the drag, sometimes a little judicious and educated thumb on the spool and don't pump the fish when it stops running. Rather than pumping the fish in the early stages keep the rod under full load, lean back and lift slowly. Any line won should be wound down on with the rod under full load.

Once the fish has been moved off the bottom, the pump and wind fighting style can return although the authors recommend a wind down and draw under load style of fighting with all reef brawlers.

## FIGHTING FISH

Fighting big tuna, marlin and sharks is a team effort. The angler turns the handle on the reel and does most of the work but someone has to drive the boat, trace, gaff and tail rope the fish.

Catching big fish regularly demands understanding and teamwork from everyone on board and learning all the little bits takes time and experience.

For anglers new to bluewater angling and those who want to learn fast a few days on a successful charter fishing boat will add rapidly to their knowledge of boat handling and big fish tactics.

Never force the fight on the trace unless necessary, always try to lead the fish to the gaff or tag pole.

The main points to remember are:

- the angler fights the fish and is kept in good position to do so by the person driving the boat.
- always use a rod bucket and a harness as soon as a big fish hooks up. This stops fatigue later in the fight.
- keep the boat down wind and down current of the fish. This stops the boat falling towards and then over the fish and the line going under the boat.
- keep the boat going slow ahead once the trace comes to hand, this keeps the fish in position for a gaff or tag shot.
- the angler halves the drag setting once the trace is in hand but is ready to move with the fish if everything cuts loose and the fight recommences.
- secure the gaff ropes before gaffing the fish or shark.
- once secured by a tail rope, leave the fish overboard until it is dead and easily handled.
- enjoy the battle or the tagging or capture of the fish, it is meant to be fun.

## FIGHTING WITH ROD AND REEL

This topic has as many variations as there are anglers however there are a couple of standard techniques which do work and anglers can add to or subtract from them as they see fit.

## PUMP AND WIND

Once a fish is hooked its usual reaction is to run somewhere. With a correctly set drag there is little an angler can or should do while the fish is running other than keep the rod bent under the load of the drag.

There is absolutely no point trying to wind line in while the fish is running.

Once the fish stops, the angler leans back with the rod and draws the fish and some line back towards the boat. This line is recovered on the down stroke with the rod.

Some pressure must be maintained against the fish during the down stroke. This is done by turning the reel handle and winding as the rod is lowered.

The rod should hold some arc of pressure at all times during the entire process.

Apart from being the most convenient way to fight a fish on rod and reel, the reason why the pump and wind technique is used is twofold. Firstly, it protects the reel which is not designed as a winch but as a place to store line and pay it back under controlled pressure.

Secondly, it helps stop line stretch from blowing the spool apart. Nylon line stretches considerably when fish are being fought and winding on the line under stretch adds some pressure to the reel spool with every turn. When this is multiplied several thousand times by every turn of line on the spool the pressure involved can be immense.

Thankfully most modern reels are extremely strong and their gearing does give them some real winding or crank power and most spools can take enormous amounts of line pressure.

Given these engineering margins it is possible to work the gear under considerable pressure without harming the reel or risking an expanded spool.

Modern fighting technique relies on some pressure being held against the fish throughout the whole pump and wind process.

On really tough fish like reef brawlers and big yellowfin tuna it is sometimes essential to fight them under almost unchanging pressure to turn them and start moving them back to the boat. During this period the angler relies on the integrity of the gear and resumes a more normal pump and wind technique once the fish is either off the bottom or is moving through the water.

On marlin, sailfish, wahoo, dolphin fish (mahi mahi) and mackerel the issue is often just keeping the line tight, slack line during a fight will usually result in the hook falling out of the fish.

Anything can happen with a big fish on a gaff. Always be prepared for an explosive finish.

With fish that jump, the aim is to wind quickly as the pressure comes off the rod. This helps keep the line tight. With both marlin and sailfish it can be impossible to keep the line tight as the fish runs and jumps in all directions, which is why so many throw the hooks early in the fight.

In this situation anglers can only work to maintain pressure with rod and reel and the skipper can help by motoring the boat away from the fish.

Wahoo and mackerel will both change direction during the fight often turning and swimming straight back towards the boat. The first time it happens the angler presumes the fish to be lost but gets a huge shock and sometimes a break off when they reel in only to have the line come tight back near the boat with a very fast moving fish on the end of it.

The trick to this fight is to never lose contact with the fish. If the line goes slack wind fast to pick up the weight again. If the hooks have been thrown then that will be rapidly obvious but keep winding until it is certain the fish is gone.

The role of the boat driver in helping to keep the line tight and the angler in position should never be underestimated. Keeping the boat going slowly ahead and then using the boat to parallel the movements of the fish is a good start.

The boat is almost always used to help pick up line lost after a big run. With the boat tracking a tangent course to the running fish. Do not drive down the same course as the fishing line this can lead to cut offs.

The other point is to not back up on fish using outboard powered vessels. Backing up is for big game boats with inboard motors. Backing up with outboards can drown and destroy them.

With outboard rigs, the fish is followed with the boat working the fish from either side or over the stern.

The only time reverse is used is to pull the boat back a few metres to pick up the trace on a tough fish or in calm water.

Anglers too need to move with their fish. This can be essential at close quarters with the fish swimming around near the boat. Standing still while the fish glides under the boat and cuts off on the hull or outboard is not a good result and is easily avoided by just walking around the boat to stay in position.

Some of these movements come from experience but most are fairly obvious. If that tender nylon touches anything while under load it will break. The angler needs to be ready to take avoidance action, fast if needs be.

The boat driver can also assist in some of these close quarters situations usually by just moving away from the fish and then repositioning the angler for another attempt to bring the fish or trace to the boat.

Most fish are handled best at boat side with the

## FACT BOX

# DON'T GET HOOKED

Being on the wrong end of a fish hook can be a painful even a frightening experience and it is usually easily avoided.

The best advice is to take particular care when handling fish because this is when the bulk of hooks ups happen.

Some fish are always difficult to handle. Dolphin fish (mahi mahi) often go berserk when landed and are best dropped into a large ice box or fish box and the lid closed. The lure or trace can be removed later. They are just as contrary when being released.

Small black and striped marlin will often come easily to the boat, particularly on heavy gear, and can be very dangerous during the release period when they suddenly awaken and do all their fighting on the trace.

Two hook type lure rigs are always a threat when releasing fish. A big sharp game hook in the hand or arm with the fish still struggling on the other hook can be a dangerous combination.

Always wear gloves and always take care when releasing fish.

Lures and rigs left lying on the floor of the boat can also be dangerous to bare feet and the hook up can produce nasty wounds.

Hooks can be removed in a number of ways or may need medical assistance if they penetrate somewhere difficult.

All hook injuries should be treated correctly to minimise damage and infection. Learn some first aid and don't rip, cut or tear anything.

If you don't know what to do or the hooked person is not happy (seriously upset) seek medical assistance.

boat going slow ahead. This keeps them in position for a gaff or tag shot.

From a moored or drifting boat it is the anglers job to fight the fish and keep the line from touching anything. This may mean doing a few laps of the boat or passing the rod and reel under the anchor rope or whatever. It is part of the learning process of fighting and landing fish.

The trick with all of this is to stay calm and cool and just go with the fish while keeping it under controlled pressure. Most fish will be landed, a few will be lost, but that in itself is part of the essence of angling. The story of the one that got away is always a classic.

## TRACING THE FISH

There are two basic ways of handling a fish near the boat and bringing it to gaff. The first is a wind on leader which allows the angler to wind the fish right to the side of the boat for gaffing or tagging. The second is to take the trace by hand and lead the fish to the gaff or tag pole.

Both systems work and the choice of either depends mostly on the angler and the way the gear is rigged.

Speaking personally, we prefer wind on traces for tuna and hand taken traces for billfish and sharks. All other game and sportfish rigs are short and the fish can be wound into range for gaffing.

When taking the trace remember its other name is a leader, it is used to lead the fish to the gaff or tag pole. Forcing any fish on the trace is almost always a recipe for disaster. Some controlled strength is used but outright force should never be needed.

The wild trace fights seen on Cairns marlin videos are best avoided for safety reasons and the fact that they can cost fish very easily. The usual tactic is to play the fish and tire it.

Gloves are worn for physical protection when tracing fish. It is possible to handle nylon traces without gloves but beware the consequences if anything goes wrong.

On billfish, at least one glove will be needed to hold the bill while the hook is removed.

On wire, gloves are absolutely essential and failure to wear them can result in serious hand injuries.

The best gloves are light leather riggers gloves but on big marlin and sharks heavy leather gloves are used with light cotton gloves underneath. This allows the heavy gloves to be slipped off if needed or if something goes wrong on the trace.

Once the double is on the reel the anglers job is to get the swivel to whoever is taking the trace. This is done very deliberately with everyone having a pre-assigned job.

With the trace in hand the angler backs off the drag a little and stays ready to clear the line and start the fight again if anything goes wrong or the fish charges away.

The fish is lead firmly and confidently to the boat and the gaff or tag is applied. Lead the fish using a hand over hand action, dropping the trace in neat coils as you go. Do not wrap the trace around your hand if possible. If a wrap is taken just take one wrap and then get another with the other hand and work the fish to the boat.

## GAFFING

Gaffing any big fish is almost always a little drama charged and it is important to do things correctly.

As the fish is drawn alongside, the person with the gaff moves in behind the trace. This is done with all fish to be gaffed, irrespective of fish size.

Being behind the trace and angler is important when gaffing any fish as it allows the person with the gaff a clean shot at the fish. If anything goes wrong, and plenty can, the fish can simply swim away and be worked back for another gaff shot.

If the person with the gaff is in front of the trace and the angler it is very easy to become tangled or hit the trace or line and break off. Avoid this situation at all costs.

Flying gaffs need to be tied off to something solid or buoyed for handling big fish.

*The right way to gaff a fish, come in behind the line or leader and place the gaff into the fish very deliberately.*

When gaffing, always aim very deliberately for a chosen spot and bring the gaff to that spot before applying the force to drive home the gaff point.

With fixed gaffs, the fish are either lifted aboard or held at the side of the boat and a tail rope is applied and the fish is secured.

Flying gaffs are pulled home with the rope held by the hand and when the gaff goes in, the pole (mostly) separates from the head. The pole is then slid back into the cockpit.

On big fish, two or three flying gaffs may be used.

Once the fish is subdued it is tail roped and lashed flush to the bollard at the stern until it is dead and easily handled.

## TAGGING

Placing a scientific tag in a fish and releasing it to fight another day is one of the fun parts of game and sportfishing.

The tags placed in fish carry a number, and a return address. On board the boat the tag comes with a data card which has the same number as the tag.

Once the fish is tagged and released it is important to complete the data card and return it to the issuing authority. Accurate measurement or estimation of the released fish is also very important.

Anglers are contributing to scientific study and some of the recaptures have shed new light on the

LEFT: A recaptured tagged kingfish is kept whole for study and measurement by scientists.

BELOW LEFT: Tagged albacore about to be released.

BELOW RIGHT: A lip hooked sailfish tagged and about to be released.

Double tagging is often done as fish do tend to shed some tags.

movements of oceanic fish and sharks.

Tagging is an interesting and satisfying use of our fish resource and it adds a socially acceptable face to sport and game fishing.

The two keys to tagging are to release the fish in good condition and careful placement of the tag.

Most fish are tagged by placing the tag high on the shoulder and into the dorsal rays. Sharks are tagged right below the dorsal fin.

The tags are angled into the tissue so they lock into the physical structure under the fins rather than just being placed in the fish's flesh.

To place the tag fight or trace the fish into position, let the fish steady itself, there is no point trying to jab a constantly moving fish.

As with gaffing, the tag spot is aimed very deliberately and the tag pole is almost touching the spot before it is jabbed forward into the fish.

Once the fish is tagged take care when removing the hooks, particularly with double hook rigged billfish lures.

Any fish that presents a danger should simply be cut free. The hooks often drop out quickly once pressure is released.

All sharks should be released by cutting the trace. Trying to remove the hooks from a shark is asking for trouble.

Speaking from personal experience, a shark bite is not painful. It is only when the local anaesthetic wears off and the stitches pump that the pain really hits you. All that blood and violated flesh doesn't do much for the day or the passengers and now we always cut the trace about 60 cm (2 ft) from the hook.

Don't fool around with sharks, even small ones can get you, although mine was a 2.5 metre (8 ft), 125 kilo (250 lb) model. The same goes for barracuda, wahoo and mackerel, their teeth are razor sharp and they will bite you.

Tagging is not an essential part of the release process either, plenty of anglers just choose to release their fish and keep only one or two for a feed. It's a matter of personal choice.

Daybreak on the bait grounds. Small boats gather to catch their live bait before proceeding to sea.

# CHAPTER 16

# LIVE BAITS—CATCHING AND RIGGING

Both live and dead baits can be a key factor in bluewater fishing. Sometimes the baits are easy to come by but at other times baits can be scarce or hard to catch. It is at these times when a little knowledge can be the difference between a good catch and a poor one.

## BAIT GROUNDS—SLIMY MACKEREL AND YELLOWTAIL

Most anglers catch their bait on recognised bait grounds. The boat anchors over a shallow reef or a protected corner known to hold bait, the berley pot is thumped a few times and up comes a cloud of yellowtail, slimy mackerel, scad or whatever.

This is the easy part. The fish are caught with a light handline fitted with a No. 6 or No. 8 Long Shank hook and a small Split shot.

If slimy mackerel are the main game and they are

Hook in back in slow drift or slow current situations

Hook under chin and out nose when drifting deep reefs

Hook from side to side when fishing baits in heavy current or when drifting fast

**Rigging live yellowtail and slimy mackerel.**

a little shy, remove the split shot and just use a slice of bait on the hook. This floats gently down and the slimies take the bait readily.

Sea garfish are usually caught the same way if they appear in the berley.

Berley is essential to the bait catching process and should never be overlooked.

Similarly, on some bait grounds it is essential to be on the right spot or you will miss out. These things need learning and come from experience in an area.

## BAIT JIGS

Sabiki type bait jigs have revolutionised the way anglers catch bait and they certainly add an extra dimension to bait catching.

3–4 kg handline
00 or 0 Split shot
No. 8 Long Shank hook
Small strips of bait

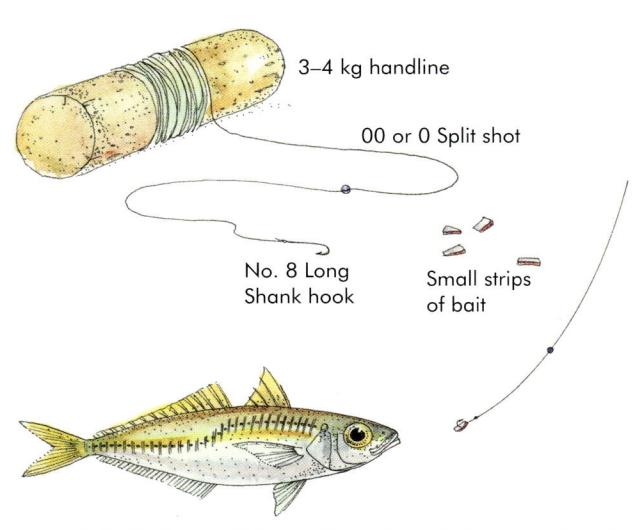

**Bait rig for catching yellowtail and slimy mackerel.**

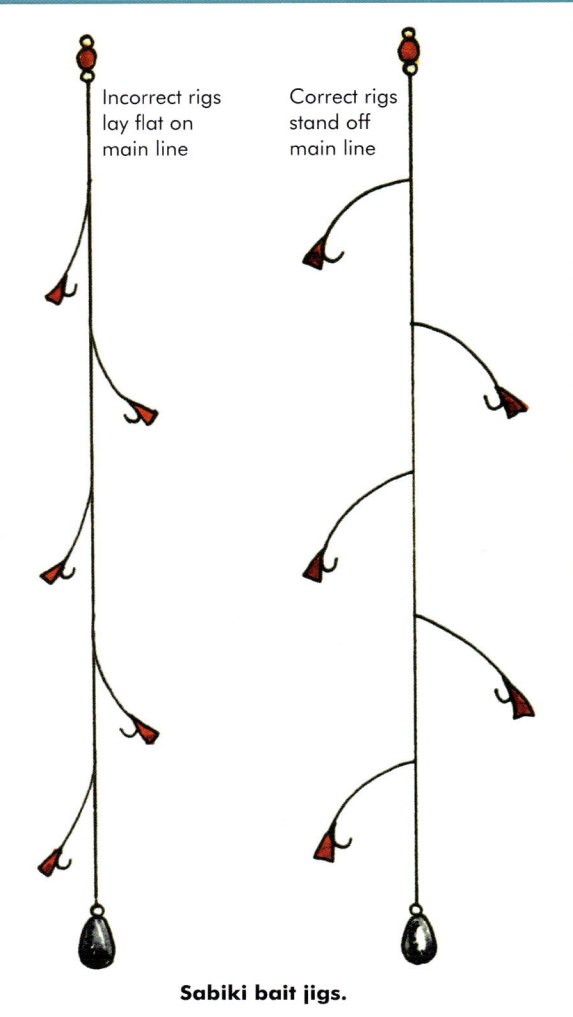

Incorrect rigs lay flat on main line

Correct rigs stand off main line

**Sabiki bait jigs.**

Slimy mackerel jigged on a Sabiki bait jig.

These strings of little jigs are rigged so they stand off the main line and can be checked for this by holding them one way and then the other in a vertical line in front of the angler.

Usually the swivel end is for attachment to the main line and the open end is for the sinker.

These jigs work best with a 30 or 60 gram (4 oz or 8 oz) sinker, even in shallow water. They are often most attractive to bait as they fall not as they rise.

They are also available in a range of sizes with size 6 being the best in most situations. The size denotes the hook size being used to make the jigs. Smaller jigs can be used if the baits needed are small. If the bait fish are a little shy on the jig, bait the hooks with little strips or cubes of fish or prawn and this will often get them biting.

Where bait jigs have really helped is their ability to catch bait from both surface schools and from schools in mid-water or on deep reefs.

Surface schools can be cast to and the jigs lifted and dropped through them to attract strikes.

For mid water or deep bait the boat is positioned over the top of the school or reef and the jig fished with an appropriate size lead for working straight up and down in the conditions, usually 120 to 180 grams (4 to 6 oz).

Once over the bait fish, the jigs are lowered to the bottom and the jigs retrieved with a lift and drop technique.

When a fish is hooked it is retrieved directly to the boat. If the jig continues to be lifted and dropped once a fish is hooked an almighty tangle will occur particularly if there are a couple of bait fish on the string.

Larger size bait jigs can also be used to catch nannygai, trevally, bonito, whiptails and other useful baits off deep reefs.

## COWANYOUNG

This southern member of the scad family is often seen rippling on the surface in big schools. It also turns up in oceanic berley slicks at times where it is easily caught with baited lines.

Most cowanyoung are caught by casting or dropping a bait jig into the school. Baited hooks or small silver lures lobbed into a school will also meet with a similar response.

Cowanyoung are an important oceanic food source and make great bait for marlin, tuna and sharks.

They will survive well in a bait tank and can be trolled in a bridle rig for several hours.

## GARFISH

Garfish can be caught on lightly weighted lines or with rod and reel and a small float. At times they may be around in big numbers and sufficient can be caught to use each day or frozen for later use.

More often they are purchased from fish shops or fish markets.

Garfish are one of the best troll baits available and are easily rigged to swim naturally through the water. These rigs may vary from single hook systems for marlin and sailfish through to ganged hooks for tailor and mackerel. (See section on Trolling Baits).

Garfish can be kept alive in a bait tank and are usually hooked under the bottom jaw in most situations where they are fished live.

Wolf herring are aggressive fish themselves but make great bait when trolled for Spanish mackerel and billfish.

Sea garfish can be caught on light tackle and frozen for later use.

## HERRING

A very wide variety of herring are used as bait for bluewater fishing.

These range from little estuary type fish to wolf herring which are up to 2 kilograms (4 lb) and used for catching both mackerel and marlin.

In some tropical areas, herring are the dominant bait fish and are caught for both bait and food.

With their silvery sides, schooling behaviour and rich, oily flesh they are a prime target for fish that eat other fish.

Most herring are caught on Sabiki type bait jigs or on light baited lines fitted with small hooks.

In areas where bait nets are legal, they can be effectively used to catch herring.

Larger herring like the wolf herring and ox eye herring (tarpon) are best caught on small lures.

Most herring do not live very long in bait tanks, so handle them carefully and use quickly after capture. The larger herring should be stored on ice or frozen for later use.

## MULLET

Small to medium sized mullet make excellent troll baits and are extremely popular in northern waters. Where available they are also an effective live bait as they are tough and survive well in the bait tank.

What mullet cannot cope with is depth. Mullet lowered past about 10 metres (30 ft) will die rapidly so they need to be fished in surface or shallow water situations.

Mullet are relatively easy to rig for trolling although the right tools are needed for removing the spine and sewing the bait.

Most mullet are purchased from bait shops but anglers in search of truly fresh baits may choose to

Slimy mackerel are best not handled just shake them from the hook into the bait tank.

Bulk boxes of pilchards are the key berley when drifting for yellowfin tuna and marlin.

Some bread or fish pulped through the berley bucket always helps to attract bait fish.

use a bait net where it is legal or catch a few with a bait line and some bread or sand worm on a No. 8 Long Shank hook.

Mullet freeze well and can be pre-rigged on shore and taken to sea for use as required. This is almost always the best method for small boat anglers.

## PIKE

Pike are a very useful bait for inshore game fish, particularly yellowtail kingfish, mulloway and Spanish mackerel.

They can be caught on bait jigs, small silver spoons or hooks baited with small whole fish like whitebait.

They will survive well in a bait tank but are a little fragile and need to be handled gently.

## PILCHARDS

Pilchards or sardines are an important bait right around the world and are used for all types of fishing.

All bluewater fish eat pilchards and they are particularly important in yellowfin tuna fishing as both bait and berley and also for mackerel, tailor and salmon fishing. They are used extensively for reef and bottom fish.

Because they are soft, pilchards do not troll very well on conventional rigs. They are usually slow trolled on ganged hook rigs with a lead head to stabilise the bait and stop it from spinning. Soft copper wire or fuse wire is used to keep the mouth of the bait shut when trolling. More classically, pilchards are fished on three and four gang hooks for tailor, salmon, bonito, yellowtail kingfish, cobia and inshore tuna.

While a few pilchards can be caught on bait jigs most are purchased in frozen blocks or in individually quick frozen (IQF) packs from bait shops.

## SALMON

Australian salmon are a popular bait, fished live for big yellowtail kingfish, trolled for marlin or drifted dead as shark baits.

They are common in both Australia and New Zealand where they are known as kahawai.

Salmon vary widely in size growing to around 5 kilograms (10 lb). In places where small salmon are abundant they are also very popular as bait. They keep very well in a bait tank and are hardy and long lived on the hook.

Most salmon are caught trolling or casting small lures or with baits like whitebait or pilchards.

Hook inserted through mouth of bait, then mouth of bait wired shut with fuse wire.

**Floating pilchard for yellowfin tuna and albacore.**

### FACT BOX

### WIRING ON A PILCHARD, OR SMALL BAIT FISH FOR BERLEY TRAIL PRESENTATION

**1.** Take pilchard, or other suitable bait fish, a short length of 0.7 mm galvanised wire (available from hardware store) and a suitable size hook rigged on a leader.

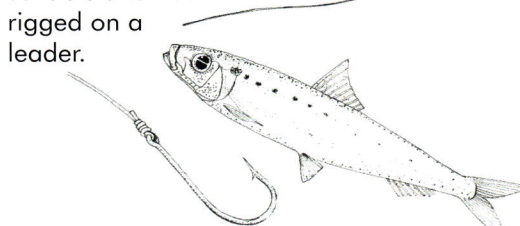

**2.** Place the hook in the bait through the gill opening.

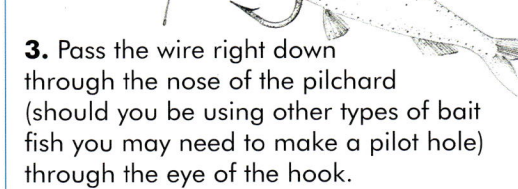

**3.** Pass the wire right down through the nose of the pilchard (should you be using other types of bait fish you may need to make a pilot hole) through the eye of the hook.

**4.** Bend one side of the wire forward so that it lays alongside the leader and wind the other around both wire and leader. Break off excess wire.

Tarpon with their shiny sides are easy to rig as swimming baits for billfish.

Small herring are often found in the estuaries.

## SMALL TUNA

Catching these little fish is an important link in the catching of larger marlin and tuna and is covered separately in the section on Trolling for Small Game Fish.

## SQUID

Squid are excellent bait for yellowtail kingfish, samson fish, cobia, broadbill swordfish, mulloway and snapper. They are also an important food for most game fish.

Despite appearing regularly in the stomach contents of all game fish, squid are rarely used as bait for them, with the exception of broadbill swordfish.

There are many reasons for this though the most important one is convenience. Live fish baits are so much simpler than mucking about with squid, and probably just as effective. It is also possible to troll rigged squid but again fish baits are easier and just as effective.

Squid are mostly caught on prawn shaped jigs which are deadly, but they also attack other live and dead baits and often cling to them long enough for a landing net to scoop them up.

Squid are very highly strung animals and die quickly after handling or capture. However, if an opportunity arises where a live or really fresh squid is available for use then it should be buttoned on at the top end of the body tube and payed out.

## TREVALLY

Small trevally turn up on bait grounds and on Sabiki jigs. These are mostly silver trevally but other types show up in tropical waters.

Their use as bait varies but they can be used very successfully. They make good baits for yellowtail kingfish, cobia and similar reef predators and will also be taken by tuna, marlin and sharks. Their flesh also makes good strip bait.

When other bait fish are scarce, trevally are a very useful standby. They are also tough and hardy and carry easily in the bait tank.

Some places (like NSW) have a size limit on trevally so be careful before throwing them in the bait tank.

## STRIP BAITS

Strip baits are slices of bait fish which are most often used to hook fish crusing in the berley slick.

The fish feeding in this situation are usually picking up scraps of berley or cut pieces of fish and accept the strips without hesitation.

The key to the presentation is to make sure the bait lays straight and does not bunch up on the hook.

Yellowtail are one of the major bait fish used by anglers.

The rig is ideal for yellowfin tuna, cobia, yellowtail kingfish, trevally, snapper and other berley feeders.

The bait is then floated back by paying out line so it falls back naturally in the current.

Strip baits are also important when bottom fishing for table fish. A slice of juicy tuna or mackerel will attract the attention of most bottom fish.

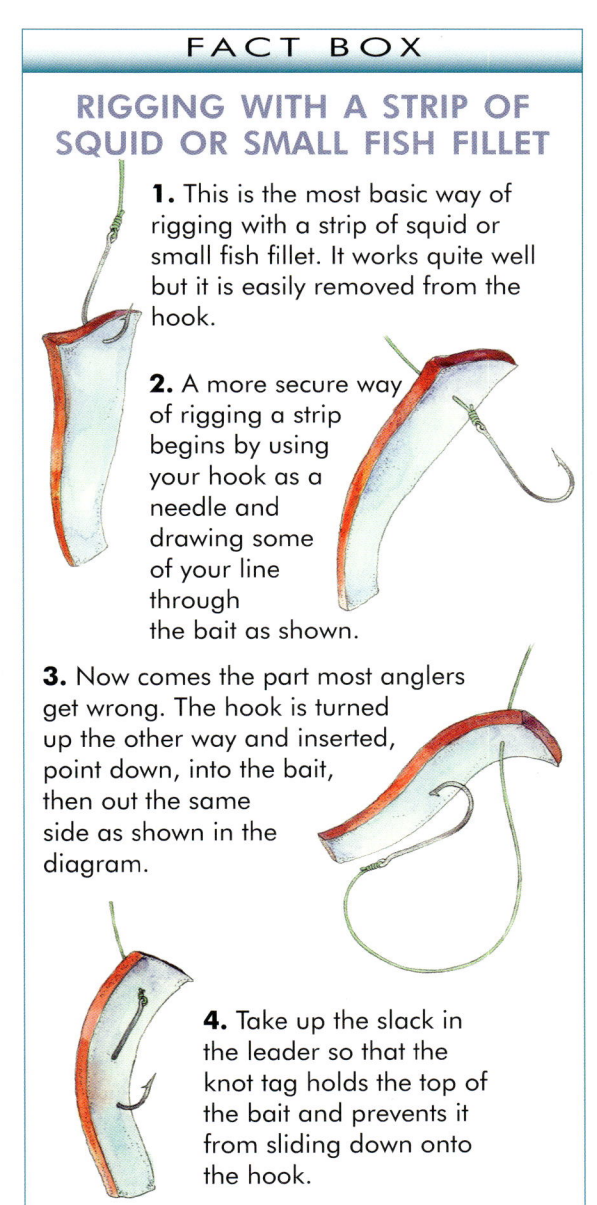

### FACT BOX

### RIGGING WITH A STRIP OF SQUID OR SMALL FISH FILLET

**1.** This is the most basic way of rigging with a strip of squid or small fish fillet. It works quite well but it is easily removed from the hook.

**2.** A more secure way of rigging a strip begins by using your hook as a needle and drawing some of your line through the bait as shown.

**3.** Now comes the part most anglers get wrong. The hook is turned up the other way and inserted, point down, into the bait, then out the same side as shown in the diagram.

**4.** Take up the slack in the leader so that the knot tag holds the top of the bait and prevents it from sliding down onto the hook.

Longfin perch or pinkies are one of the sea's great treats.

# CHAPTER 17

# Enjoying the Catch

Quality fresh fish is one of the most enjoyable and healthy by-products of a day's fishing.

By all means release fish if you wish but the sheer pleasure of a good fish meal shared with family and friends should never be overlooked.

Fishing, like all things in life needs a sense of balance. A day spent marlin fishing might yield a few tagged billfish but there may also be tuna, wahoo, dolphin fish (mahi mahi), mackerel or whatever also coming to the boat.

It is always possible a fish destined for release will come to the boat badly injured or even dead. You have no control over this and tail wrapped or shark mauled fish will either come in dead or die soon after capture.

If you want a feed of fish take some. It is the essence of going fishing anyway. The politically correct can take a leap. Both black and striped marlin are good eating. Blue marlin are not good eating. All of the tunas and smaller game fish are good to eat. Some are exceptional.

If you are going to eat the fish the first step is to have ice and appropriate size storage space. Without ice, storing game fish is useless so don't be scared to carry plenty of it.

Kill the fish quickly to prevent it thrashing around and bruising itself.

Lay the fish as flat and straight as possible and cover it in ice. With marlin, take the photographs, cut off the head and tail and drop the trunk onto ice. The trunk can also be halved for easy storage if need be.

Barbequed wahoo cutlets with a little Cajun seasoning takes some beating.

ABOVE: Insulated, zip or velcro closing bags are available for large game fish like marlin and tuna. Just add plenty of ice to keep the fish in prime condition.

ABOVE: Cobia are great table fish.

BELOW: Cleaning large fish takes sharp knives and a little skill to remove the best cuts of meat.

Once back in port the best way to handle the fish is to either fillet or cutlet the catch depending on personal preference.

Big fish like tuna and marlin are usually halved above the anal fin, then cut to the spine lengthwise along the bloodline and filleted off.

The result yields long, boneless circular pieces which are very easy to prepare for the table.

Wash the fish, pack the pieces in plastic bags and put them back in a chilled container with plenty of ice.

The last part of the process is to learn how to cook the fish. There are dozens of books on the subject and if the main ingredient is free there will be plenty of chances to get things right.

Some people just know how to cook, some of us need to learn. Your authors have learned the cooking and eating side of fishing adds an extra dimension to their sport and provides superb food and taste sensations available only to anglers.

Nobody has access to fresher fish than us. Learn to use it and enjoy it but never waste it.

LEFT: If you catch it and kill it make sure you have the tools to clean it and prepare it properly for the table.

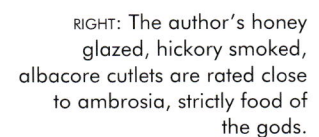

RIGHT: The author's honey glazed, hickory smoked, albacore cutlets are rated close to ambrosia, strictly food of the gods.

# CHAPTER 18

# SPECIES

## BILLFISH SPECIES

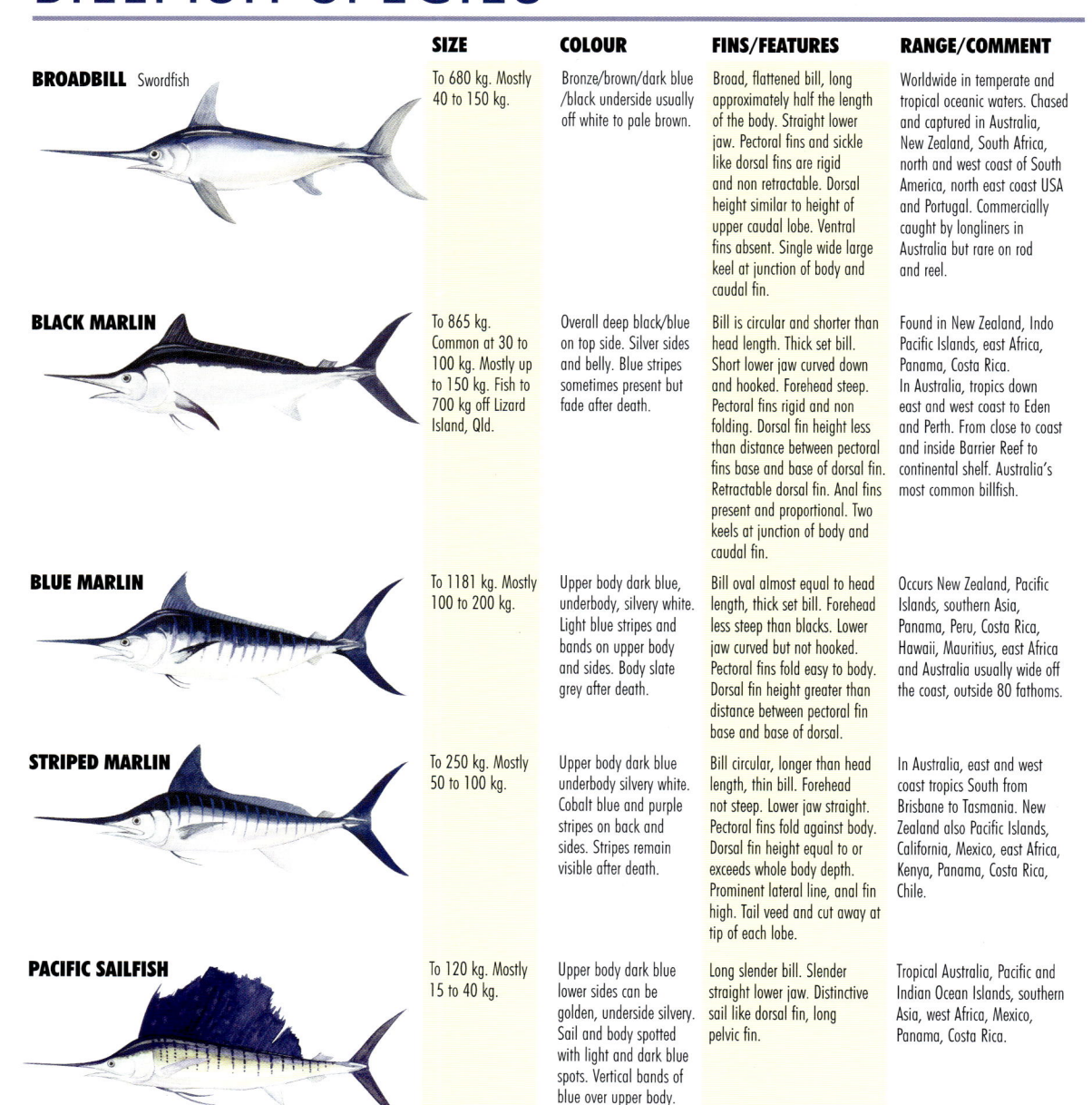

| | SIZE | COLOUR | FINS/FEATURES | RANGE/COMMENT |
|---|---|---|---|---|
| **BROADBILL** Swordfish | To 680 kg. Mostly 40 to 150 kg. | Bronze/brown/dark blue/black underside usually off white to pale brown. | Broad, flattened bill, long approximately half the length of the body. Straight lower jaw. Pectoral fins and sickle like dorsal fins are rigid and non retractable. Dorsal height similar to height of upper caudal lobe. Ventral fins absent. Single wide large keel at junction of body and caudal fin. | Worldwide in temperate and tropical oceanic waters. Chased and captured in Australia, New Zealand, South Africa, north and west coast of South America, north east coast USA and Portugal. Commercially caught by longliners in Australia but rare on rod and reel. |
| **BLACK MARLIN** | To 865 kg. Common at 30 to 100 kg. Mostly up to 150 kg. Fish to 700 kg off Lizard Island, Qld. | Overall deep black/blue on top side. Silver sides and belly. Blue stripes sometimes present but fade after death. | Bill is circular and shorter than head length. Thick set bill. Short lower jaw curved down and hooked. Forehead steep. Pectoral fins rigid and non folding. Dorsal fin height less than distance between pectoral fins base and base of dorsal fin. Retractable dorsal fin. Anal fins present and proportional. Two keels at junction of body and caudal fin. | Found in New Zealand, Indo Pacific Islands, east Africa, Panama, Costa Rica. In Australia, tropics down east and west coast to Eden and Perth. From close to coast and inside Barrier Reef to continental shelf. Australia's most common billfish. |
| **BLUE MARLIN** | To 1181 kg. Mostly 100 to 200 kg. | Upper body dark blue, underbody, silvery white. Light blue stripes and bands on upper body and sides. Body slate grey after death. | Bill oval almost equal to head length, thick set bill. Forehead less steep than blacks. Lower jaw curved but not hooked. Pectoral fins fold easy to body. Dorsal fin height greater than distance between pectoral fin base and base of dorsal. | Occurs New Zealand, Pacific Islands, southern Asia, Panama, Peru, Costa Rica, Hawaii, Mauritius, east Africa and Australia usually wide off the coast, outside 80 fathoms. |
| **STRIPED MARLIN** | To 250 kg. Mostly 50 to 100 kg. | Upper body dark blue underbody silvery white. Cobalt blue and purple stripes on back and sides. Stripes remain visible after death. | Bill circular, longer than head length, thin bill. Forehead not steep. Lower jaw straight. Pectoral fins fold against body. Dorsal fin height equal to or exceeds whole body depth. Prominent lateral line, anal fin high. Tail veed and cut away at tip of each lobe. | In Australia, east and west coast tropics South from Brisbane to Tasmania. New Zealand also Pacific Islands, California, Mexico, east Africa, Kenya, Panama, Costa Rica, Chile. |
| **PACIFIC SAILFISH** | To 120 kg. Mostly 15 to 40 kg. | Upper body dark blue lower sides can be golden, underside silvery. Sail and body spotted with light and dark blue spots. Vertical bands of blue over upper body. | Long slender bill. Slender straight lower jaw. Distinctive sail like dorsal fin, long pelvic fin. | Tropical Australia, Pacific and Indian Ocean Islands, southern Asia, west Africa, Mexico, Panama, Costa Rica. |

SPECIES  133

| | SIZE | COLOUR | FINS/FEATURES | RANGE/COMMENT |
|---|---|---|---|---|
| **SHORTBILL SPEARFISH**  | To 45 kg. | Upper body dark blue, lower body silvery white. No stripes present. | Bill very short, slightly larger than lower jaw. Lower jaw slender and straight. Pectoral fins narrow and short. First dorsal fin high, long and curved at rear. | Common in Hawaii, also other Pacific Islands, California and Australia's temperate east coast. |

# SHARK SPECIES

| | SIZE | COLOUR | FINS/FEATURES | RANGE/COMMENT |
|---|---|---|---|---|
| **HAMMERHEAD SHARK** 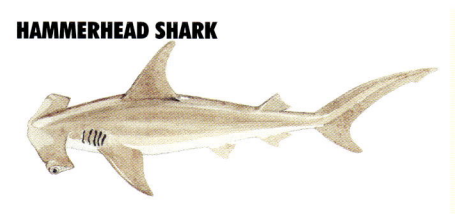 | To 550 kg. Mostly 25 to 100 kg. | Generally upper body is bronze grey and lower body white, though there is variation between species. | All 9 species (4 in Australia) display a flattened, expanded hammerhead shape. There are 5 short gill slits. The caudal fin is non lunate in shape. Hammerhead teeth are small broad based triangles with their edges faintly serrated. | In all warm and temperate fisheries, extending from large rivers and bays out to open ocean. Australia, New Zealand, east coast USA, east and west coast of Africa, Gulf of Mexico. |
| **MAKO SHARK** Blue Pointer, Mackerel Shark.  | To 700 kg. Mostly 30 to 100 kg. | Upper body cobalt blue lower body silvery white. | Pointed snout and large black eyes. Well defined caudal keel and lobes of the caudal fin almost equal. Five long gill slits. Closely related to the white shark, the mako has teeth that are more dagger like and not flattened. | Open ocean species distributed worldwide in tropical and temperate seas. Particularly in Australia, New Zealand, South Africa, east and west coast USA, South America and Pacific Islands. |
| **WHITE SHARK** White Pointer, White Death, Great White.  | To 2275 kg. Size highly variable. | Upper body light to dark grey to blue/grey. Lower body white, the boundary between the upper and lower colours usually distinctive. Pectoral fins usually have black tips or dusky appearance. | Conical snout, black eye, five long gill slits. Distinct keel at junction of caudal fin and body. Broad, flattened trangular shaped teeth with serrations. Teeth shape and body colour used to distinguish it from mako. | More prominent in temperate seas of southern Australia. North east USA, South Africa, Nova Scotia, California and New Zealand South Island. Now protected in Australia. |
| **BLUE SHARK** Blue Whaler.  | To 230 kg. Most 30 to 100 kg. | Upper body cobalt to indigo blue, lower body white. | Long slim body and large pectoral fins dusky at tips. Dark eye circled in white. No keel at junction of body and caudal fin. Five short gill slits. Has long, narrow snout, upper teeth relatively narrow, hook shaped, triangular and finely serrated. | Open ocean species in tropical and temperate seas. All Australian waters except Arafura Sea, Gulf of Carpentaria and Torres Strait. Also New Zealand, north east coast of USA, California, England, Portugal and the Azores. |
| **TIGER SHARK**  | To 820 kg. Mostly 100 to 300 kg. | Upper body is grey to blue/grey. Lower body is white. The back and sides have a pattern of dark vertical bars and blotches. | The body is stout, particularly forward of the first dorsal fin. Head is large and broad and snout short and blunt. Upper caudal fin lobe tapering to thin pointed tip. Teeth similar shape to rooster comb and heavily serrated. | Common in tropical and temperate seas. Found from coastal bays and rivers to oceanic waters. Around reefs and islands and reef channels. Around eastern and western Australia, New Zealand North Island, east and western South Africa, Florida and Pacific Islands. |
| **THRESHER SHARK**  | To 450 kg. Mostly 30 to 100 kg . | Upper body is blue/green/grey. Lower body white sides and belly often mottled. | The long upper lobe of the caudal fin (tail) is a distinguishing feature, being about as long as the body. Teeth are relatively small, narrowly triangular and smooth edged. Second dorsal and anal fins are very small. | Common in cooler temperate seas. Occurs north east USA, New Zealand, Australia—most common in eastern Victoria and occasionally caught in warmer waters of the other states, California, Spain and Portugal. |

# BLUEWATER FISHING

| | SIZE | COLOUR | FINS/FEATURES | RANGE/COMMENT |
|---|---|---|---|---|
| **GREY NURSE SHARK**  | To 250 kg. | Dirty greyish brown above shading to dull white below. Reddish brown spots on the tail and posteria half of body. | Large stout shark with both dorsal and anal fins of similar size. Eyes yellow with a black pupil. Caudal fin is asymmetrical, broad and floppy. Teeth awl shaped and long. | Recorded in all Australian states except Tasmania. Tropical and temperate parts of north and south Atlantic, Indian and Western Pacific Oceans, Australia and South Africa. Protected species in Australia, rarely caught by recreational anglers |
| **WHALER SHARK**  | To 500 kg. Wide size range depending on species. | Because of diversity of species (49) large variation in colour. Upper body can be black, bronze, grey, copper and usually cream or white below. | Upper lobe of tail much longer than lower. Eye yellowish with small pupil. Generally first dorsal much larger than second. Teeth are wide in upper jaw and narrow in lower. Both are slightly serrated. It is the shape and distribution of teeth that is the key factor in identifying the different species. | From upper reaches of estuaries to open ocean. Worldwide distribution in tropical to temperate waters. Large numbers in Australia, New Zealand, South Africa, Indo Pacific, north east coast USA, Florida. |

# LARGE TUNA SPECIES

| | SIZE | COLOUR | FINS/FEATURES | RANGE/COMMENT |
|---|---|---|---|---|
| **YELLOWFIN TUNA** Ahi (Hawaii)  | To 110 kg in Australia. Up to 120 kg in Hawaii. To 175 kg in USA and Mexico west coast. Mostly 20 to 60 kg. | Deep blue/black on back. Bright yellow dorsal and anal fins and yellow finlets. Tones of olive and yellow along body. Juveniles have marked bands on belly. | Fish from about 20 kg upwards have elongated 2nd dorsal and anal fins (known as sickles) growing longer and more curved with size. Long pectoral fins. Caudal keel yellow. | Worldwide distribution in temperate and tropical seas. In Australia—east and west coast, most common from Mooloolaba to Gabo Island, Northern New Zealand, South Africa, east Borneo and Pacific Islands. |
| **BIG EYE TUNA**  | To 200 kg. Mostly 40 to 100 kg. | Deep blue/black on back. Some olive and yellow on body. Fins not as bright yellow as yellowfin tuna. | Dorsal and anal fins do not elongate as with yellowfin. Barrel shaped, much stockier than yellowfin. Liver of bigeye tuna always striated in colour, liver of yellowfin is uniform in colour. Pectoral fins shorter than yellowfin. Dark caudal keel. Prominent large eye. | Worldwide in temperate and tropical waters. Common on Atlantic US coast and Australian east coast. Almost always found wide out over the 200 fathom drop off. Very few are caught by recreational anglers as they are nocturnal and found wide off the coast. |
| **SOUTHERN BLUE TUNA**  | To 160 kg. Mostly 20 to 60 kg. | Deep blue/black on top with silver blue sides. | Pectoral fins short, second dorsal and anal fins short. Finlets yellow edged in black. Caudal keel yellow. | Southern Australia particularly southern W.A., S.A., Bass Strait and Tasmania. Also southern New Zealand and South Africa. Seriously threatened by commercial over fishing. |
| **DOGTOOTH TUNA**  | To 135 kg. Mostly 10 to 45 kg. | Purple to blue/black on top with silver sides. | Very large peg shaped teeth. Prominently marked lateral line. No scales on body. Pectoral fins short. This tuna is unmistakable due to its teeth. | Found in tropical Australia, east Africa and Pacific Islands particularly around deep coral drop offs, in passes between reefs, over submerged reef and bommies. |
| **LONGTAIL TUNA** Northern Bluefin Tuna (Australia).  | To 40 kg. Average fish 10 to 20 kg. | Blue/black top and silvery sides. | Long body shape, finer build than most tuna. Long pectoral fins. Caudal keel dark, finlets yellow with grey edges. | East and west coast of Australia and also in Indo-Pacific region and across Arabian Gulf. Along Asian coast. |

SPECIES    135

| | SIZE | COLOUR | FINS/FEATURES | RANGE/COMMENT |
|---|---|---|---|---|
| **GIANT BLUEFIN** 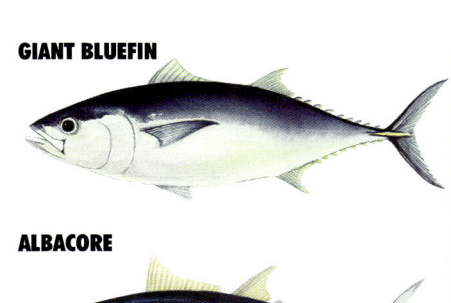 | To 800 kg. | Upper body blue/black with silvery sides. | Short pectoral fins, second dorsal and anal fins short. Finlets yellow edged in black. Caudal keel black. | Mostly a Mediterranean and Atlantic Ocean species although a population exists in the north Pacific off California. Caught occasionally off Australian east coast and New Zealand. |
| **ALBACORE** 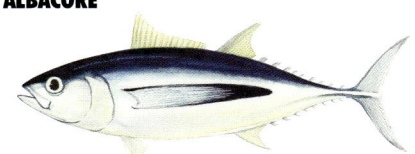 | To 45 kg. Average fish 7 to 15 kg. | Black topside with iridescent blue stripe along middle of body. This fades after death. Silvery white undersides. | The very long strap like pectoral fins are highly distinctive. Most fins are dark with a white edge on the tail. Large eye is also a clear indicator. | Common in New Zealand, Hawaii, west coast USA and east coast of Australia from Tasmania to Brisbane in waters deeper than 60 fathoms. |

# SMALL TUNA SPECIES

| | SIZE | COLOUR | FINS/FEATURES | RANGE/COMMENT |
|---|---|---|---|---|
| **STRIPED TUNA** Skipjack Tuna, Oceanic Bonito.  | To 35 kg. 12 kg max in Australia. Average fish 2 to 8 kg. Very large fish to 25 kg regularly caught in north Pacific and around Hawaii. | Purple/black back with electric blue lines near tail end of back. Silver/white sides with 4 to 6 dark stripes on belly and underside. | Short pectoral fins. Tail and finlets black. Short chunky shape. | A worldwide distribution in tropical and temperate seas. Ranges from shore to over the shelf. In Australia common along both the east and west coast. Most common of all the tuna world wide. |
| **MACKEREL TUNA** Kawa Kawa, Little Tuna.  | To 15 kg. Average size 2 to 10 kg. | Back is blue green with distinctive mackerel pattern on lower back. Silvery white sides. Three to five spots on belly below pectoral fins. | Fins short with black tail. | Worldwide species found predominantly inshore around reefs, islands and coastal bays. Rarely found wide offshore. |
| **FRIGATE MACKEREL**  | To 3kg. Average 500 grams to 1.5 kg. | Back is blue/black with blotched mackerel pattern, bright silvery sides. | Fins short. Eye is larger compared to mackerel tuna. No dots under pectoral fins. | A common bait species in temperate waters of Australia and South America. |
| **WATSON'S LEAPING BONITO**  | To 4 kg. Average 1 to 2 kg. | Upper body green with distinctive check pattern. Edges with tint of yellow. | First dorsal very high and black. | Mostly a tropical and warm water fish. This fish is most common along Australian east coast and tropical Pacific Islands. |
| **BONITO** Horse Mackerel, Pacific Bonito.  | To 11 kg. Average 2 to 5 kg. | Upper body blue/green full length grey/black stripes along body, fins black. | Fins short tail black. Dorsal fin long, distinctive teeth. | Bonito are a common inshore and reef fish found in most tropical and temperate seas. Usually found around reefs, headlands bommies, deep bays and similar structures. |

# TREVALLY SPECIES

| | SIZE | COLOUR | FINS/FEATURES | RANGE/COMMENT |
|---|---|---|---|---|
| **GREAT TREVALLY** | To 50 kg. Usually 5 to 20 kg. | Dark blue/green on topside shading to yellow/green and then silvery. Colours can vary. | The large eye is prominent and the bull shaped head, deep body and strong conical teeth are distinctive. Heavy tail scutes run along the sides. | Found throughout the tropics of Australia and in western Pacific and Indian Oceans. Found on inshore and coral bommies, reef edges and in channels through reefs. Juveniles regularly encountered in estuaries. |
| **TURRUM** | To 15 kg. Usually 3 to 10 kg. | Opalescent blue topsides and silver below. There are usually colour blotches along sides. | Fins have a yellow hue. Body is elongated more than GT's. | This fish rarely ranges away from coral country preferring warmer waters. In Australia mostly found north of Fraser Island and Shark Bay. |
| **GOLDEN TREVALLY** | To 35 kg. Usually 3 to 15 kg. | Small fish distinctive golden yellow with dark bars. Large fish less distinctive but always with some yellow colouration and black bands through the eye areas. | Fins light coloured with yellow shades. This trevally has no teeth. All other large trevally have teeth. | Found around reefs and coral throughout the Pacific and Indian Oceans. Most common north of Morton Bay, Qld Australia. Larger fish often found on deeper reef edges. |
| **QUEENFISH** Giant Leatherskin. | To 15 kg. Usually 3 to 8 kg. | Silvery green with brass to yellow hues. Five to 8 circular blotches located above the lateral line. | Tail is deeply forked. Dorsal and anal fins are large and sweep back. Mouth and head shape are unmistakable. | Found in the western Pacific, throughout Asia and down the Indian Ocean side of Africa. Common in tropical seas, rarely found south of north Topics. |

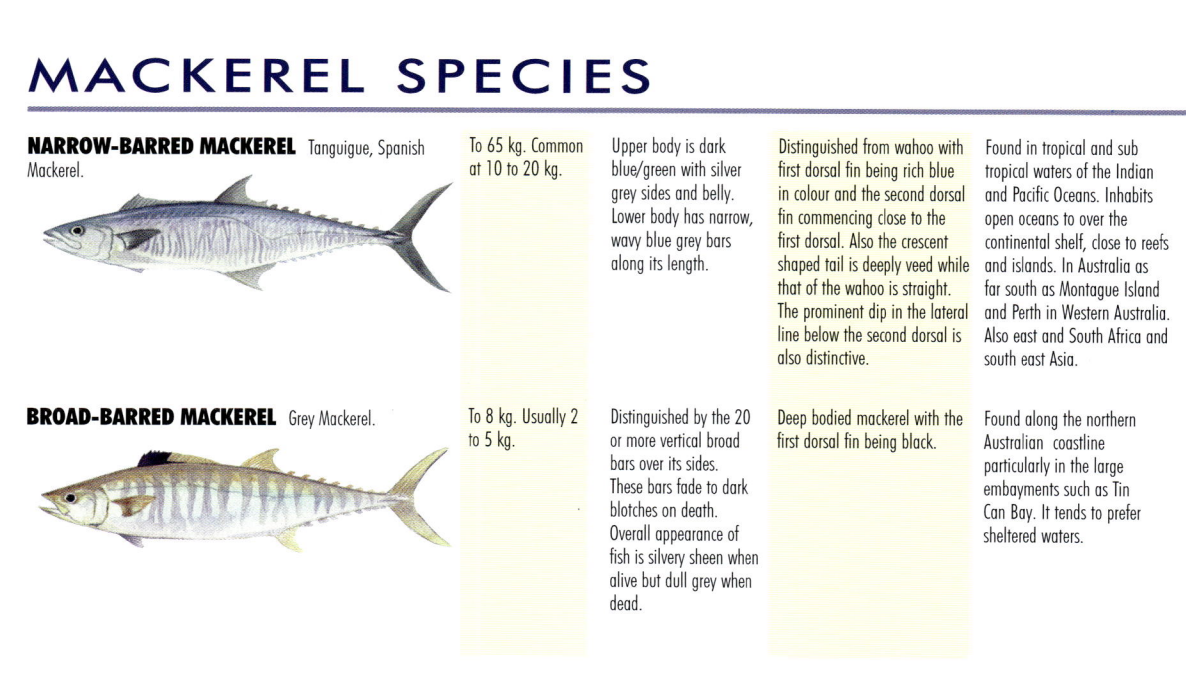

# MACKEREL SPECIES

| | SIZE | COLOUR | FINS/FEATURES | RANGE/COMMENT |
|---|---|---|---|---|
| **NARROW-BARRED MACKEREL** Tanguigue, Spanish Mackerel. | To 65 kg. Common at 10 to 20 kg. | Upper body is dark blue/green with silver grey sides and belly. Lower body has narrow, wavy blue grey bars along its length. | Distinguished from wahoo with first dorsal fin being rich blue in colour and the second dorsal fin commencing close to the first dorsal. Also the crescent shaped tail is deeply veed while that of the wahoo is straight. The prominent dip in the lateral line below the second dorsal is also distinctive. | Found in tropical and sub tropical waters of the Indian and Pacific Oceans. Inhabits open oceans to over the continental shelf, close to reefs and islands. In Australia as far south as Montague Island and Perth in Western Australia. Also east and South Africa and south east Asia. |
| **BROAD-BARRED MACKEREL** Grey Mackerel. | To 8 kg. Usually 2 to 5 kg. | Distinguished by the 20 or more vertical broad bars over its sides. These bars fade to dark blotches on death. Overall appearance of fish is silvery sheen when alive but dull grey when dead. | Deep bodied mackerel with the first dorsal fin being black. | Found along the northern Australian coastline particularly in the large embayments such as Tin Can Bay. It tends to prefer sheltered waters. |

# SPECIES 137

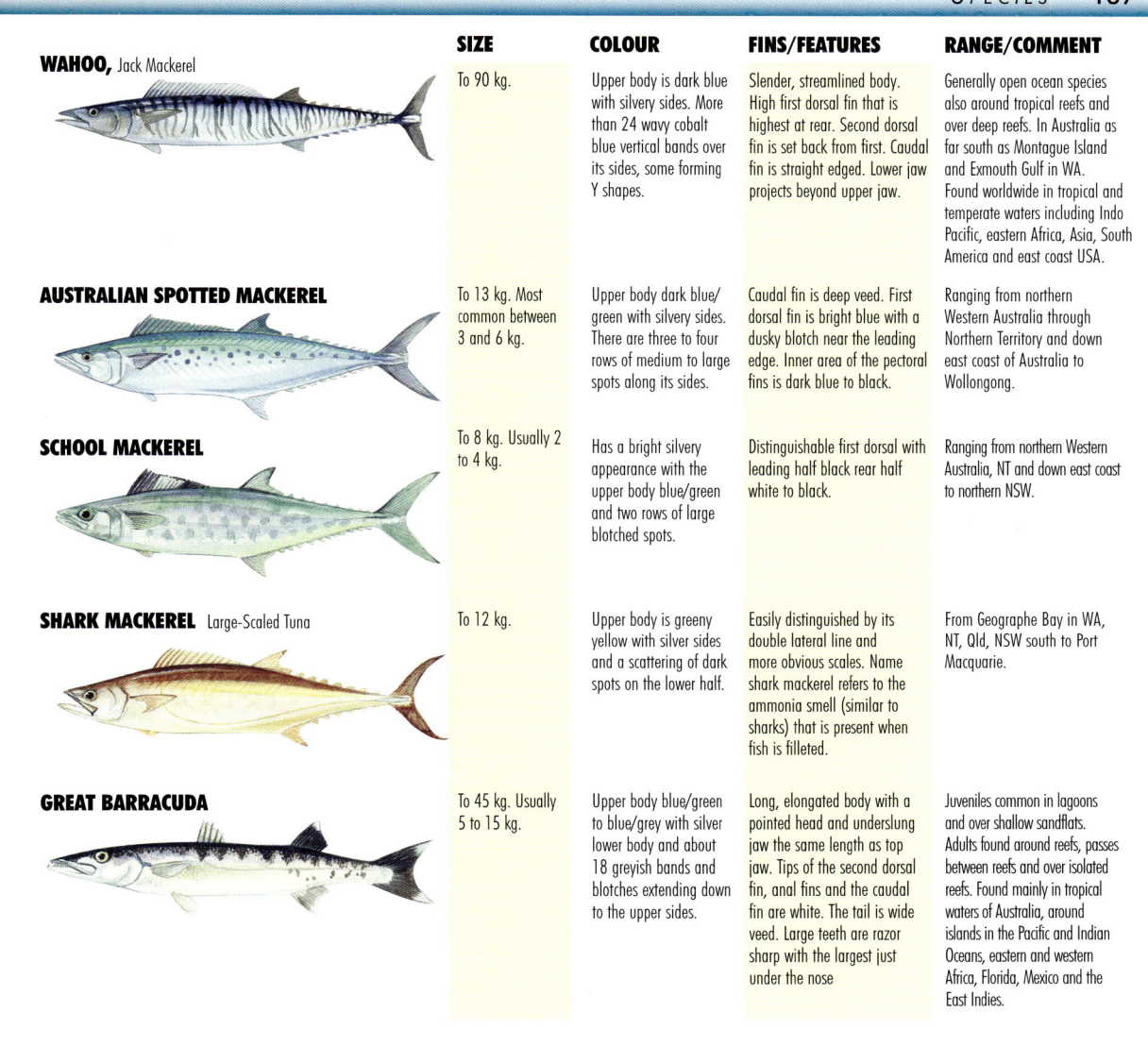

| | SIZE | COLOUR | FINS/FEATURES | RANGE/COMMENT |
|---|---|---|---|---|
| **WAHOO,** Jack Mackerel | To 90 kg. | Upper body is dark blue with silvery sides. More than 24 wavy cobalt blue vertical bands over its sides, some forming Y shapes. | Slender, streamlined body. High first dorsal fin that is highest at rear. Second dorsal fin is set back from first. Caudal fin is straight edged. Lower jaw projects beyond upper jaw. | Generally open ocean species also around tropical reefs and over deep reefs. In Australia as far south as Montague Island and Exmouth Gulf in WA. Found worldwide in tropical and temperate waters including Indo Pacific, eastern Africa, Asia, South America and east coast USA. |
| **AUSTRALIAN SPOTTED MACKEREL** | To 13 kg. Most common between 3 and 6 kg. | Upper body dark blue/green with silvery sides. There are three to four rows of medium to large spots along its sides. | Caudal fin is deep veed. First dorsal fin is bright blue with a dusky blotch near the leading edge. Inner area of the pectoral fins is dark blue to black. | Ranging from northern Western Australia through Northern Territory and down east coast of Australia to Wollongong. |
| **SCHOOL MACKEREL** | To 8 kg. Usually 2 to 4 kg. | Has a bright silvery appearance with the upper body blue/green and two rows of large blotched spots. | Distinguishable first dorsal with leading half black rear half white to black. | Ranging from northern Western Australia, NT and down east coast to northern NSW. |
| **SHARK MACKEREL** Large-Scaled Tuna | To 12 kg. | Upper body is greeny yellow with silver sides and a scattering of dark spots on the lower half. | Easily distinguished by its double lateral line and more obvious scales. Name shark mackerel refers to the ammonia smell (similar to sharks) that is present when fish is filleted. | From Geographe Bay in WA, NT, Qld, NSW south to Port Macquarie. |
| **GREAT BARRACUDA** | To 45 kg. Usually 5 to 15 kg. | Upper body blue/green to blue/grey with silver lower body and about 18 greyish bands and blotches extending down to the upper sides. | Long, elongated body with a pointed head and underslung jaw the same length as top jaw. Tips of the second dorsal fin, anal fins and the caudal fin are white. The tail is wide veed. Large teeth are razor sharp with the largest just under the nose | Juveniles common in lagoons and over shallow sandflats. Adults found around reefs, passes between reefs and over isolated reefs. Found mainly in tropical waters of Australia, around islands in the Pacific and Indian Oceans, eastern and western Africa, Florida, Mexico and the East Indies. |

# LIGHT GAME FISH

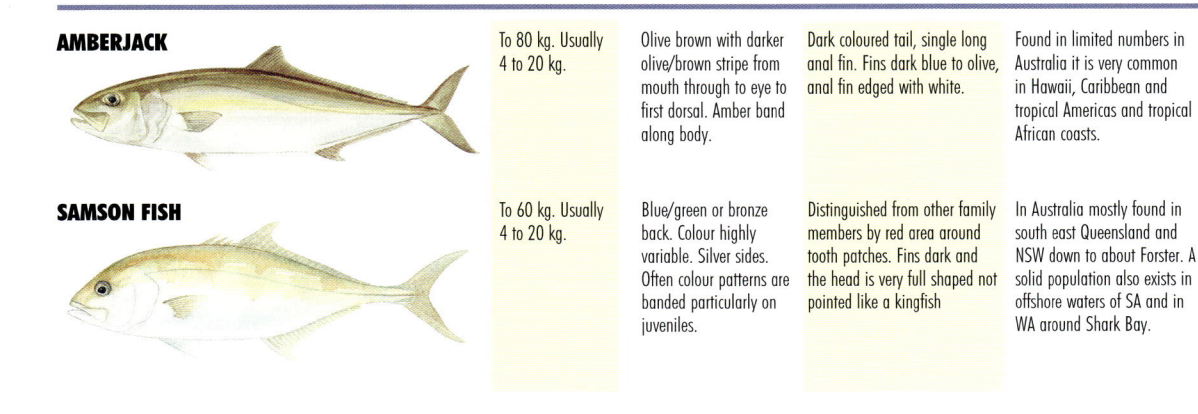

| | SIZE | COLOUR | FINS/FEATURES | RANGE/COMMENT |
|---|---|---|---|---|
| **AMBERJACK** | To 80 kg. Usually 4 to 20 kg. | Olive brown with darker olive/brown stripe from mouth through to eye to first dorsal. Amber band along body. | Dark coloured tail, single long anal fin. Fins dark blue to olive, anal fin edged with white. | Found in limited numbers in Australia it is very common in Hawaii, Caribbean and tropical Americas and tropical African coasts. |
| **SAMSON FISH** | To 60 kg. Usually 4 to 20 kg. | Blue/green or bronze back. Colour highly variable. Silver sides. Often colour patterns are banded particularly on juveniles. | Distinguished from other family members by red area around tooth patches. Fins dark and the head is very full shaped not pointed like a kingfish | In Australia mostly found in south east Queensland and NSW down to about Forster. A solid population also exists in offshore waters of SA and in WA around Shark Bay. |

| | SIZE | COLOUR | FINS/FEATURES | RANGE/COMMENT |
|---|---|---|---|---|
| **YELLOWTAIL KINGFISH** | To 70 kg. Usually 3 to 15 kg. | Blue/green on top with prominent yellow stripe along body. White underbody and sides. | Distinctive yellow tail and fins. No teeth only rough tooth pads. | Found in coastal waters from shore to 100 fathoms. Common in temperate seas of Australia and New Zealand, California and South Africa. Also in southern Japan. |
| **RAINBOW RUNNER** Hawaiian Salmon. | To 20 kg. Usually 3 to 8 kg. | Blue/green top, sides with blue and yellow side band, Silvery white beneath. | Tail is yellow and deeply forked. Mouth is small and soft. | Found in tropical and temperate waters in Pacific and Indian Oceans. Common around coral drop offs and reefs and near flotsam also common around offshore islands. |
| **COBIA** Crab Eater, Black Kingfish. | To 70 kg. Usually 5 to 20 kg. | Upper body dark brown with two cream coloured side lines. Lighter brown underneath and cream belly. | Body shape is similar to a shark or remora. Head is flattened and tail is broad and powerful. This distinctive fish is easily identified. | Tropical and temperate seas in Australia, Africa, Asia and Caribbean. |
| **MAHI MAHI** Dolphin Fish, Dorado. | To 45 kg. Usually 3 to 15 kg. | Upper body electric blue with silver blue sides. Fish turns gold with flashes of green during capture. | A very distinctive looking fish. Males have a prominent high upright head. The dorsal fin is high and runs almost full length along the body. | Worldwide fish in tropical and temperate waters. Highly prized as a sport and food fish in most areas where it is common. Often present in large numbers. |

# APPENDIX

## FIVE MOST COMMON KNOTS

While there are whole books on the subject, it may surprise some anglers that most bluewater anglers can get by with four or five knots.

We work two charter boats and use a total of five knots all up. Learn these well and you will be able to cope with almost any situation.

The main trick with knots is to tie them properly, wet them down as they are pulled tight to minimise line burning friction and be confident in the knot, it will help when the fish are being fought.

Our essential knots are the Locked Blood knot, Uni knot, Plaited Double, Albright Special and the Dropper Loop.

## A ROD RIGGED RIGHT

Game rods and many sportfishing rods are rigged with a plaited double at the end, tied to a quality snap swivel or wind on trace. The double provides a section of line for holding and controlling fish when they are close to the boat. It can be really handy when trying to get particularly tough fish to the boat or when bringing the trace to hand. The double adds a strength area when chasing fish that jump like marlin and which can land on the line during big leaps.

Finally a double line provides extra strength at the knot which is vital when chasing big fish.

This system is then complemented by carrying all the lures, shark, marlin and other traces in pre-rigged form with an eye, swivel or ring ready to attach to the snap swivel.

When the boat starts trolling the lures are clipped on and payed out. When the boat stops the lures are disconnected and the shark, marlin or tuna traces can be attached, baited and payed out. Yellowtail kingfish traces or whatever can be similarly pre-rigged and clipped on and off as required. It's a great system and it works well. The only change comes in some forms of yellowfin tuna fishing where the swivel is clipped off the end of the double and the yellowfin traces are connected directly to remove any metal from the system.

A similar system to the double is often adopted for lighter sportfishing rigs although many of these use a small swivel and one metre or more length of nylon trace to the snap swivel rather than a double. It is a matter of personal choice on the lighter gear although a double is still handy and some sort of trace is essential in almost all situations.

Having the rod rigged correctly and set up to handle whatever comes along adds to catches by enabling quick changes to tackle whatever fish may appear. It also adds confidence that the gear is right when a really big fish hooks up.

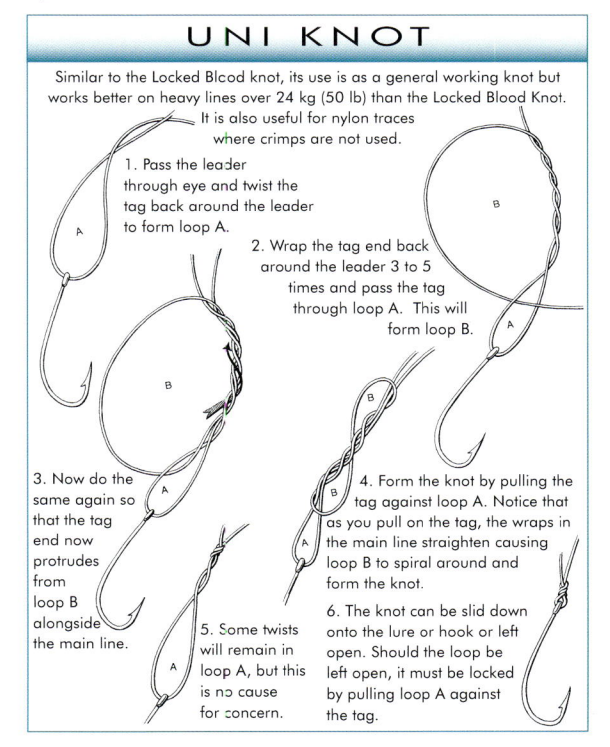

## LOCKED BLOOD KNOT

A good general working knot used in all types of rigs. It is a safe secure knot that is totally reliable.

1. Thread the eye of your hook or swivel and twist the tag and main line together.

2. Complete three to six twists and thread the tag back through the first twist. The heavier your line, the less twists you will use.

3. Pull the line so that the knot begins to form. Do not pull it tight yet or you will have an un-locked half blood knot which may slip should you be tying new line to a shiny metal surface.

4. To lock the knot, thread the tag through the open loop which has formed at the top of the knot.

5. Pull the knot firmly and the result should be something like this. Should a loop form within the knot, simply pull the tag until it disappears.

## UNI KNOT

Similar to the Locked Blood knot, its use is as a general working knot but works better on heavy lines over 24 kg (50 lb) than the Locked Blood Knot. It is also useful for nylon traces where crimps are not used.

1. Pass the leader through eye and twist the tag back around the leader to form loop A.

2. Wrap the tag end back around the leader 3 to 5 times and pass the tag through loop A. This will form loop B.

3. Now do the same again so that the tag end now protrudes from loop B alongside the main line.

4. Form the knot by pulling the tag against loop A. Notice that as you pull on the tag, the wraps in the main line straighten causing loop B to spiral around and form the knot.

5. Some twists will remain in loop A, but this is no cause for concern.

6. The knot can be slid down onto the lure or hook or left open. Should the loop be left open, it must be locked by pulling loop A against the tag.

## PLAITED DOUBLE

The Plaited Double is an essential part of any game fishing rig. Although it looks a little complicated, it is in fact easy to tie and its role in the handling and successful landing of big fish should not be underestimated. The Spider Hitch provides a quick and reliable double for spin and sportfishing rigs but a Plaited Double or Bimini Twist is the best bet for game fishing.

1. Measure off just over twice the length of line your finished double will be. The main line or standing part is A. The returning length is B, and the tag is C. Let's call the loop D.

2. Your rod should be firmly in the rod holder and the clutch of the reel set. Keeping the line tight by pulling away from your rod and reel, pass C over B (alongside A). Pull B tight. Because tension must be maintained throughout the plaiting process, it helps to wrap each successive leg in turn, around your finger as shown.

3. Pass A over C and pull C tight.

4. Pass B over A and pull A tight.

5. Pass C over B and pull C tight. Having completed the first cycle of the plait, increase tension on the line, even though some distortion may appear.

6. Now you are getting the idea, A goes over B. Then C pulled tight.

7. Plait lengths are 5 cm for 10 kg, 8 cm for 15 kg, 12 cm for 24 kg. Double the tag over to form loop E as shown.

8. Loop E is plaited in just like the other two single legs. I secure the loop against the plait with the thumb and forefinger of the right hand as shown.

9. Transfer loop E to the index finger or your left hand and cross leg B over it to the centre. Now pull E tight.

10. Pass A over B and pull B tight.

11. Pass E over A and pull A tight.

12. B goes over E, pull E tight.

13. A has already gone over B, shown is E over A.

14. Shown is A over B.

15. Continue for one complete cycle of the plait then pass loop D through loop E.

16. Then pull the entire double through.

17. Secure the double by pulling on loop D against tag C to form a collar around the double.

## DROPPER LOOP

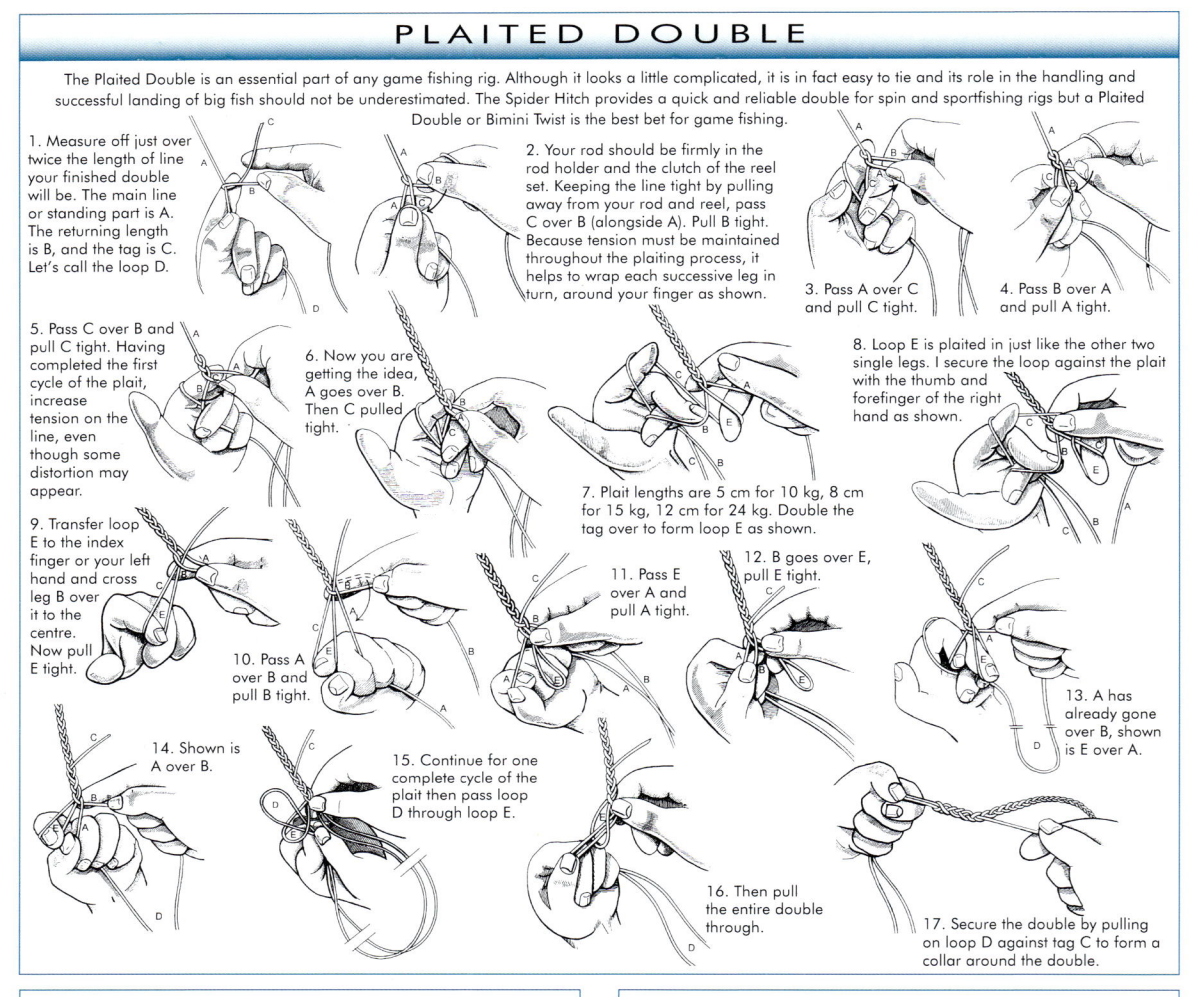

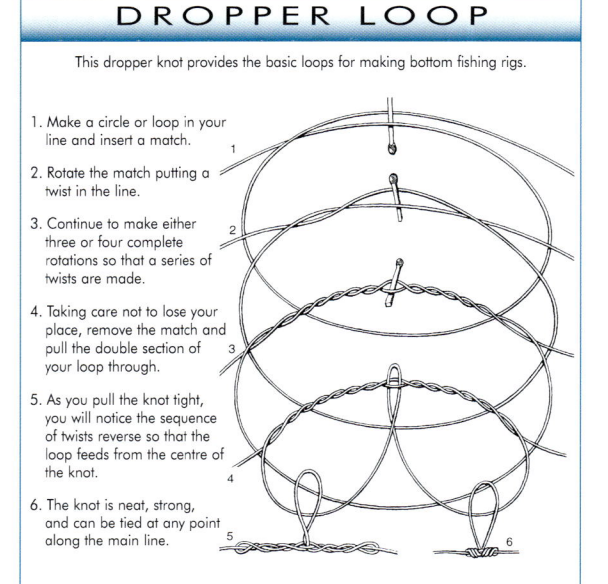

This dropper knot provides the basic loops for making bottom fishing rigs.

1. Make a circle or loop in your line and insert a match.

2. Rotate the match putting a twist in the line.

3. Continue to make either three or four complete rotations so that a series of twists are made.

4. Taking care not to lose your place, remove the match and pull the double section of your loop through.

5. As you pull the knot tight, you will notice the sequence of twists reverse so that the loop feeds from the centre of the knot.

6. The knot is neat, strong, and can be tied at any point along the main line.

## IMPROVED ALBRIGHT

This essential knot is used for joining nylon traces to the doubles of game reels. This enables the trace to be wound onto the reel and allows fish to be wound right to the gaff without touching the trace. The same knot can also be used for attaching nylon coated wire to the double.

1. Double the heavier monofilament leader and thread the lighter line through, then around, the resulting loop.

2. Continue wrapping down the loop in the heavier monofilament leader with the lighter monofilament line.

3. Make five wraps down the loop then back up the other direction over the first wraps.

4. Complete five wraps in each direction and thread the tag back through the loop.

5. Partially close the knot first with gentle pressure on the main line and tag of both leader and line.

6. When the knot begins to tighten, let both the tag of the line, and the tag leader, go. Then tighten.

7. Close the knot and trim the tags.